75 Seafood Recipes for Home

By: Kelly Johnson

Table of Contents

Fish Recipes:
- Grilled Lemon Garlic Salmon
- Baked Cod with Herbs
- Teriyaki Glazed Mahi-Mahi
- Pan-Seared Tilapia with Lemon Butter Sauce
- Cajun Blackened Catfish
- Pesto Crusted Halibut
- Coconut Lime Grilled Snapper
- Mediterranean Stuffed Branzino
- Crispy Baked Haddock
- Lemon Dill Grilled Swordfish

Shrimp Recipes:
- Garlic Butter Shrimp Scampi
- Cajun Shrimp and Sausage Skillet
- Coconut Curry Shrimp
- Lemon Garlic Butter Shrimp Skewers
- Honey Sriracha Shrimp Stir-Fry
- Grilled Chimichurri Shrimp
- Shrimp and dBroccoli Alfredo
- Bang Bang Shrimp Tacos
- Garlic Parmesan Baked Shrimp
- Spicy Thai Shrimp Salad

Scallop Recipes:
- Pan-Seared Scallops with White Wine Sauce
- Bacon-Wrapped Scallops
- Lemon Garlic Butter Scallops
- Scallop and Asparagus Risotto
- Coconut Curry Scallop Stir-Fry
- Herb-Crusted Baked Scallops
- Scallop and Corn Chowder
- Grilled Scallop and Mango Skewers
- Scallops with Brown Butter and Sage
- Scallop and Avocado Ceviche

Crab Recipes:
- Crab Stuffed Mushrooms
- Creamy Crab and Spinach Dip

- Old Bay Crab Cakes
- Garlic Butter Roasted Crab Legs
- Crab and Corn Chowder
- Crab Rangoon
- Spicy Crab Linguine
- Avocado and Crab Salad
- Grilled Crab Quesadillas
- Cajun Crab Boil

Lobster Recipes:

- Lobster Mac and Cheese
- Lobster Bisque
- Grilled Lobster Tails with Garlic Butter
- Lobster Roll
- Lobster and Shrimp Paella
- Lobster and Avocado Salad
- Lobster and Asparagus Risotto
- Lobster Newberg
- Lobster and Mango Salsa Tacos
- Lobster Thermidor

Mixed Seafood Recipes:

- Seafood Paella
- Cioppino (Italian Seafood Stew)
- Seafood Gumbo
- Thai Seafood Curry
- Mediterranean Seafood Pasta
- Seafood Enchiladas
- Seafood Stir-Fry with Vegetables
- Seafood Tostadas
- Seafood Kabobs with Lemon Garlic Marinade
- Seafood and Saffron Risotto

Fish Tacos:

- Grilled Fish Tacos with Cilantro Lime Slaw
- Baja-Style Fish Tacos
- Spicy Mango Fish Tacos
- Blackened Fish Tacos with Avocado Crema
- Beer-Battered Fish Tacos
- Sriracha Mayo Fish Tacos
- Grilled Mahi-Mahi Tacos with Pineapple Salsa
- Cajun Shrimp Tacos with Slaw
- Chipotle Lime Salmon Tacos

- Teriyaki Glazed Tuna Tacos

Soups and Salads Recipes:
- Seafood Chowder
- Thai Coconut Seafood Soup
- Mediterranean Fish Soup
- Brazilian Moqueca (Fish Stew)
- Spicy Seafood Ramen

Fish Recipes:
Grilled Lemon Garlic Salmon

Ingredients:

- 4 salmon fillets
- 3 tablespoons olive oil
- 3 cloves garlic, minced
- Zest of 1 lemon
- Juice of 1 lemon
- 1 teaspoon dried oregano
- Salt and pepper to taste
- Lemon slices for garnish
- Fresh chopped parsley for garnish

Instructions:

Prepare the Marinade:
- In a bowl, whisk together olive oil, minced garlic, lemon zest, lemon juice, dried oregano, salt, and pepper.

Marinate the Salmon:
- Place the salmon fillets in a shallow dish or a resealable plastic bag.
- Pour the marinade over the salmon, making sure each fillet is coated evenly.
- Allow the salmon to marinate for at least 30 minutes in the refrigerator. For a more intense flavor, you can marinate it for up to 2 hours.

Preheat the Grill:
- Preheat your grill to medium-high heat.

Grill the Salmon:
- Remove the salmon from the marinade and let any excess drip off.
- Place the salmon fillets on the preheated grill, skin side down.
- Grill for about 4-5 minutes per side, or until the salmon easily flakes with a fork. Cooking time may vary based on the thickness of the fillets.

Basting:
- While grilling, you can baste the salmon with any remaining marinade to enhance the flavor.

Serve:
- Once the salmon is cooked through, transfer it to a serving platter.
- Garnish with lemon slices and freshly chopped parsley.

Enjoy:
- Serve the Grilled Lemon Garlic Salmon with your favorite side dishes, such as steamed vegetables, rice, or a fresh salad.

This recipe delivers a delightful combination of grilled smokiness, zesty lemon, and savory garlic. It's a perfect dish for a quick and flavorful meal!

Baked Cod with Herbs

Ingredients:

- 4 salmon fillets
- 3 tablespoons olive oil
- 3 cloves garlic, minced
- Zest of 1 lemon
- Juice of 1 lemon
- 1 teaspoon dried oregano
- Salt and pepper to taste
- Lemon slices for garnish
- Fresh chopped parsley for garnish

Instructions:

Prepare the Marinade:
- In a bowl, whisk together olive oil, minced garlic, lemon zest, lemon juice, dried oregano, salt, and pepper.

Marinate the Salmon:
- Place the salmon fillets in a shallow dish or a resealable plastic bag.
- Pour the marinade over the salmon, making sure each fillet is coated evenly.
- Allow the salmon to marinate for at least 30 minutes in the refrigerator. For a more intense flavor, you can marinate it for up to 2 hours.

Preheat the Grill:
- Preheat your grill to medium-high heat.

Grill the Salmon:
- Remove the salmon from the marinade and let any excess drip off.
- Place the salmon fillets on the preheated grill, skin side down.
- Grill for about 4-5 minutes per side, or until the salmon easily flakes with a fork. Cooking time may vary based on the thickness of the fillets.

Basting:
- While grilling, you can baste the salmon with any remaining marinade to enhance the flavor.

Serve:
- Once the salmon is cooked through, transfer it to a serving platter.
- Garnish with lemon slices and freshly chopped parsley.

Enjoy:
- Serve the Grilled Lemon Garlic Salmon with your favorite side dishes, such as steamed vegetables, rice, or a fresh salad.

This recipe delivers a delightful combination of grilled smokiness, zesty lemon, and savory garlic. It's a perfect dish for a quick and flavorful meal!

Baked Cod with Herbs

Ingredients:

- 4 cod fillets
- 3 tablespoons olive oil
- 2 tablespoons fresh lemon juice
- 2 cloves garlic, minced
- 1 teaspoon dried oregano
- 1 teaspoon dried thyme
- Salt and pepper to taste
- Lemon wedges for serving
- Fresh chopped parsley for garnish

Instructions:

Preheat the Oven:
- Preheat your oven to 400°F (200°C).

Prepare the Marinade:
- In a small bowl, whisk together the olive oil, lemon juice, minced garlic, dried oregano, dried thyme, salt, and pepper.

Marinate the Cod:
- Place the cod fillets in a baking dish or on a lined baking sheet.
- Brush the fillets with the prepared herb marinade, ensuring they are evenly coated on both sides.

Bake the Cod:
- Bake the cod in the preheated oven for about 12-15 minutes or until the fish is opaque and easily flakes with a fork. Cooking time may vary based on the thickness of the fillets.

Broil for Crispy Top (Optional):
- If you desire a slightly crispy top, you can broil the cod for an additional 2-3 minutes, keeping a close eye to prevent burning.

Serve:
- Transfer the baked cod to serving plates.
- Garnish with fresh chopped parsley and serve with lemon wedges on the side.

Enjoy:
- Enjoy your Baked Cod with Herbs with your favorite side dishes like roasted vegetables, quinoa, or a simple salad.

This recipe brings out the natural flavors of the cod while infusing it with the aromatic blend of herbs. It's a healthy and tasty option for a quick dinner.

Pan-Seared Tilapia with Lemon Butter Sauce

Ingredients:

For the Tilapia:

- 4 tilapia fillets
- Salt and pepper to taste
- 1 teaspoon paprika
- 2 tablespoons olive oil

For the Lemon Butter Sauce:

- 4 tablespoons unsalted butter
- 3 tablespoons fresh lemon juice
- 2 cloves garlic, minced
- 1 teaspoon dried parsley (or 1 tablespoon fresh parsley), chopped
- Salt and pepper to taste

Instructions:

Season the Tilapia:
- Pat the tilapia fillets dry with paper towels.
- Season both sides of each fillet with salt, pepper, and paprika.

Preheat the Pan:
- Heat olive oil in a large skillet over medium-high heat.

Pan-Sear the Tilapia:
- Place the tilapia fillets in the hot skillet, skin side up.
- Sear for about 3-4 minutes on each side or until the fish is golden brown and easily flakes with a fork.

Prepare the Lemon Butter Sauce:
- In a separate small saucepan, melt the butter over medium heat.
- Add minced garlic and sauté for about 1 minute until fragrant.

Combine Ingredients:
- Stir in fresh lemon juice and dried parsley. Season the sauce with salt and pepper to taste.

Pour Sauce Over Tilapia:
- Pour the lemon butter sauce over the pan-seared tilapia fillets.

Serve:
- Transfer the tilapia fillets to serving plates.
- Spoon some of the lemon butter sauce over each fillet.

Garnish and Enjoy:
- Garnish with additional fresh parsley if desired.
- Serve immediately, and enjoy your Pan-Seared Tilapia with Lemon Butter Sauce with your preferred side dishes like rice, steamed vegetables, or a salad.

This recipe offers a perfect balance of flavors, with the pan-seared tilapia complemented by the rich and zesty lemon butter sauce. It's a quick and delightful dish for any meal.

Cajun Blackened Catfish

Ingredients:

For the Cajun Spice Mix:

- 1 tablespoon paprika
- 1 teaspoon dried thyme
- 1 teaspoon dried oregano
- 1 teaspoon onion powder
- 1 teaspoon garlic powder
- 1 teaspoon cayenne pepper (adjust to taste)
- 1 teaspoon black pepper
- 1 teaspoon salt

For the Catfish:

- 4 catfish fillets
- 4 tablespoons unsalted butter, melted
- Lemon wedges for serving
- Chopped fresh parsley for garnish (optional)

Instructions:

Prepare Cajun Spice Mix:
- In a bowl, combine all the Cajun spice mix ingredients - paprika, thyme, oregano, onion powder, garlic powder, cayenne pepper, black pepper, and salt. Mix well.

Coat Catfish Fillets:
- Pat the catfish fillets dry with paper towels.
- Coat each fillet generously with the Cajun spice mix, pressing the spices onto both sides of the fillets.

Preheat the Skillet:
- Heat a cast-iron skillet or a heavy-bottomed pan over medium-high heat.

Blacken the Catfish:
- Brush each side of the catfish fillets with melted butter.
- Place the fillets in the hot skillet and cook for about 3-4 minutes on each side or until the fish is blackened and easily flakes with a fork.

Serve:
- Transfer the blackened catfish to serving plates.

Garnish and Enjoy:

- Garnish with lemon wedges and chopped fresh parsley if desired.
- Serve immediately and enjoy your Cajun Blackened Catfish with sides like rice, coleslaw, or roasted vegetables.

This Cajun blackened catfish recipe provides a bold and spicy flavor that perfectly complements the mild taste of catfish. It's a quick and impressive dish for those who enjoy a touch of heat in their meals.

Pesto Crusted Halibut

Ingredients:

For the Pesto:

- 2 cups fresh basil leaves, packed
- 1/2 cup grated Parmesan cheese
- 1/2 cup pine nuts
- 3 cloves garlic, peeled
- 1/2 cup extra-virgin olive oil
- Salt and pepper to taste

For the Halibut:

- 4 halibut fillets (6-8 ounces each)
- Salt and pepper to taste
- 2 tablespoons olive oil
- 1/2 cup Panko breadcrumbs (optional for added crunch)

Instructions:

Prepare the Pesto:

    Combine Ingredients:
- In a food processor, combine basil, Parmesan cheese, pine nuts, and garlic. Pulse until finely chopped.

    Add Olive Oil:
- With the food processor running, gradually add the olive oil in a steady stream until the pesto reaches a smooth consistency.

    Season:
- Season the pesto with salt and pepper to taste. Set aside.

Prepare the Halibut:

    Preheat the Oven:
- Preheat your oven to 400°F (200°C).

    Season the Halibut:
- Pat the halibut fillets dry with paper towels. Season both sides with salt and pepper.

    Pan-Sear the Halibut:
- Heat olive oil in an oven-safe skillet over medium-high heat.

- Sear the halibut fillets for about 2 minutes on each side, or until they have a golden crust.

Apply Pesto and Breadcrumbs:
- If using Panko breadcrumbs for added crunch, spread a thin layer on top of each halibut fillet.
- Spoon a generous amount of pesto over each fillet, spreading it evenly.

Bake in the Oven:
- Transfer the skillet to the preheated oven and bake for approximately 10-12 minutes or until the halibut is cooked through and flakes easily.

Serve:
- Remove from the oven and let it rest for a few minutes.
- Serve the Pesto Crusted Halibut on plates, and drizzle any remaining pesto from the skillet over the top.

Garnish and Enjoy:
- Garnish with fresh basil leaves or a sprinkle of Parmesan if desired.
- Enjoy your Pesto Crusted Halibut with your favorite side dishes, such as roasted vegetables, quinoa, or a light salad.

This recipe showcases the rich flavors of halibut complemented by the vibrant and aromatic pesto crust. It's a delightful dish that's both elegant and easy to prepare.

Coconut Lime Grilled Snapper

Ingredients:

For the Marinade:

- 1 cup coconut milk
- Zest and juice of 2 limes
- 3 tablespoons soy sauce
- 2 tablespoons fish sauce
- 2 tablespoons brown sugar
- 1 tablespoon minced ginger
- 2 cloves garlic, minced
- 1 teaspoon red chili flakes (adjust to taste)
- Salt and pepper to taste

For the Snapper:

- 4 snapper fillets (about 6-8 ounces each), skin-on
- 2 tablespoons coconut oil (for brushing the grill)
- Fresh cilantro for garnish
- Lime wedges for serving

Instructions:

Prepare the Marinade:

　Whisk Marinade Ingredients:
- In a bowl, whisk together coconut milk, lime zest, lime juice, soy sauce, fish sauce, brown sugar, minced ginger, minced garlic, red chili flakes, salt, and pepper. Ensure that the brown sugar is dissolved.

　Marinate the Snapper:
- Place the snapper fillets in a shallow dish or a resealable plastic bag.
- Pour the marinade over the snapper, making sure each fillet is well coated.
- Marinate in the refrigerator for at least 30 minutes, allowing the flavors to infuse.

Grill the Snapper:

　Preheat the Grill:
- Preheat your grill to medium-high heat.

Brush with Coconut Oil:
- Brush the grill grates with coconut oil to prevent sticking.

Grill the Snapper:
- Remove the snapper from the marinade, letting excess drip off.
- Place the fillets on the preheated grill, skin side down.
- Grill for about 4-5 minutes per side or until the snapper is cooked through and has a nice grill mark.

Baste with Marinade:
- During grilling, baste the snapper with some of the remaining marinade for added flavor.

Serve:
- Transfer the grilled snapper fillets to a serving platter.

Garnish and Enjoy:
- Garnish with fresh cilantro and serve with lime wedges on the side.
- Enjoy your Coconut Lime Grilled Snapper with your choice of sides, such as coconut rice or a fresh salad.

This recipe offers a delightful combination of coconut, lime, and grilled flavors, creating a tropical and refreshing dish. It's perfect for a summer barbecue or any time you want a taste of the tropics!

Mediterranean Stuffed Branzino

Ingredients:

For the Branzino:

- 2 whole branzino, cleaned and scaled
- Salt and pepper to taste
- 2 tablespoons olive oil
- 1 lemon, thinly sliced
- Fresh thyme sprigs for garnish

For the Stuffing:

- 1 cup cherry tomatoes, halved
- 1/2 cup Kalamata olives, pitted and sliced
- 1/4 cup red onion, finely chopped
- 2 cloves garlic, minced
- 2 tablespoons capers
- 2 tablespoons fresh parsley, chopped
- 2 tablespoons fresh oregano, chopped
- 2 tablespoons olive oil
- Salt and pepper to taste

Instructions:

Prepare the Stuffing:

    Combine Ingredients:
- In a bowl, mix together cherry tomatoes, Kalamata olives, red onion, minced garlic, capers, chopped parsley, chopped oregano, olive oil, salt, and pepper. Set aside.

Prepare the Branzino:

    Preheat the Oven:
- Preheat your oven to 400°F (200°C).

    Season the Branzino:
- Pat the branzino dry with paper towels. Season the inside and outside of each fish with salt and pepper.

    Stuff the Branzino:
- Stuff each branzino cavity with the prepared Mediterranean stuffing mixture.

Secure with Toothpicks:
- Use toothpicks to secure the opening of each fish, ensuring that the stuffing stays inside.

Arrange in Baking Dish:
- Place the stuffed branzino in a baking dish.

Drizzle with Olive Oil:
- Drizzle olive oil over the top of each stuffed branzino.

Add Lemon Slices:
- Arrange lemon slices on top of the fish.

Bake in the Oven:
- Bake in the preheated oven for about 20-25 minutes or until the branzino is cooked through and flakes easily with a fork.

Serve:
- Carefully transfer the stuffed branzino to serving plates.

Garnish and Enjoy:
- Garnish with fresh thyme sprigs.
- Serve immediately, and enjoy your Mediterranean Stuffed Branzino with your favorite sides like roasted vegetables or couscous.

This recipe combines the freshness of branzino with the vibrant flavors of the Mediterranean, creating a dish that's both visually appealing and incredibly flavorful. It's a perfect choice for a special dinner or entertaining guests.

Crispy Baked Haddock

Ingredients:

- 4 haddock fillets (about 6-8 ounces each)
- 1 cup breadcrumbs (Panko or regular)
- 1/4 cup grated Parmesan cheese
- 1 teaspoon dried parsley
- 1/2 teaspoon garlic powder
- 1/2 teaspoon onion powder
- 1/2 teaspoon paprika
- Salt and pepper to taste
- 1/4 cup melted butter or olive oil
- Lemon wedges for serving
- Fresh chopped parsley for garnish

Instructions:

Preheat the Oven:
- Preheat your oven to 400°F (200°C). Line a baking sheet with parchment paper or lightly grease it.

Prepare the Coating:
- In a shallow bowl, combine breadcrumbs, Parmesan cheese, dried parsley, garlic powder, onion powder, paprika, salt, and pepper. Mix well.

Coat the Haddock:
- Pat the haddock fillets dry with paper towels.
- Dip each fillet into the melted butter or olive oil, ensuring both sides are coated.
- Press the haddock fillets into the breadcrumb mixture, coating them evenly on all sides. Place the coated fillets on the prepared baking sheet.

Bake in the Oven:
- Bake the haddock in the preheated oven for about 15-20 minutes or until the fish is cooked through and the coating is golden and crispy. Cooking time may vary based on the thickness of the fillets.

Serve:
- Carefully transfer the crispy baked haddock to serving plates.

Garnish and Enjoy:
- Garnish with fresh chopped parsley and serve with lemon wedges on the side.

- Enjoy your Crispy Baked Haddock with your favorite sides like roasted vegetables, mashed potatoes, or a light salad.

This recipe gives you a flavorful and crispy coating on the outside while keeping the haddock tender and flaky on the inside. It's a fantastic option for a quick and satisfying seafood dinner.

Lemon Dill Grilled Swordfish

Ingredients:

For the Swordfish Marinade:

- 4 swordfish steaks (about 6-8 ounces each)
- 1/4 cup olive oil
- Zest and juice of 1 lemon
- 2 tablespoons fresh dill, chopped
- 2 cloves garlic, minced
- 1 teaspoon Dijon mustard
- Salt and pepper to taste

For Garnish:

- Lemon wedges
- Fresh dill sprigs

Instructions:

Prepare the Swordfish Marinade:
- In a bowl, whisk together olive oil, lemon zest, lemon juice, chopped dill, minced garlic, Dijon mustard, salt, and pepper.

Marinate the Swordfish:
- Place the swordfish steaks in a shallow dish or a resealable plastic bag.
- Pour the marinade over the swordfish, making sure each steak is well-coated.
- Marinate in the refrigerator for at least 30 minutes to let the flavors infuse.

Preheat the Grill:
- Preheat your grill to medium-high heat.

Grill the Swordfish:
- Remove the swordfish from the marinade, letting any excess drip off.
- Place the swordfish steaks on the preheated grill.
- Grill for about 4-5 minutes per side or until the fish is cooked through and has a nice grill mark. Cooking time may vary based on the thickness of the steaks.

Baste with Marinade (Optional):
- Optionally, you can baste the swordfish with some of the remaining marinade during grilling for added flavor.

Serve:

- Carefully transfer the grilled swordfish to serving plates.

Garnish and Enjoy:
- Garnish with lemon wedges and fresh dill sprigs.
- Serve immediately, and enjoy your Lemon Dill Grilled Swordfish with your preferred side dishes, such as quinoa, couscous, or a fresh salad.

This recipe highlights the robust flavors of swordfish complemented by the zesty and herbaceous combination of lemon and dill. It's a perfect dish for a light and refreshing seafood meal.

Shrimp Recipes:

Garlic Butter Shrimp Scampi

Ingredients:

- 1 pound large shrimp, peeled and deveined
- Salt and black pepper to taste
- 8 ounces linguine or spaghetti
- 4 tablespoons unsalted butter
- 4 tablespoons olive oil
- 4 cloves garlic, minced
- 1/2 teaspoon red pepper flakes (adjust to taste)
- Zest of 1 lemon
- Juice of 1 lemon
- 1/2 cup chicken broth or white wine
- 1/4 cup fresh parsley, chopped
- Grated Parmesan cheese for serving (optional)

Instructions:

Prepare the Shrimp:
- Pat the shrimp dry with paper towels. Season with salt and black pepper.

Cook the Pasta:
- Cook the linguine or spaghetti according to the package instructions until al dente. Drain and set aside.

Sauté the Shrimp:
- In a large skillet, heat 2 tablespoons of butter and 2 tablespoons of olive oil over medium-high heat.
- Add the shrimp to the skillet and cook for about 2 minutes per side or until they turn pink and opaque. Remove the shrimp from the skillet and set aside.

Make the Garlic Butter Sauce:
- In the same skillet, add the remaining butter and olive oil.
- Add minced garlic and red pepper flakes. Sauté for about 1 minute until the garlic becomes fragrant but not browned.

Deglaze with Liquid:
- Pour in the chicken broth or white wine to deglaze the pan, scraping up any flavorful bits from the bottom.

Combine Pasta and Shrimp:
- Add the cooked pasta to the skillet and toss to coat in the garlic butter sauce.
- Return the cooked shrimp to the skillet.

Add Lemon Zest and Juice:
- Stir in the lemon zest and lemon juice. Toss everything together to combine.

Finish and Garnish:
- Sprinkle chopped parsley over the top and toss once more to incorporate.
- Optionally, sprinkle with grated Parmesan cheese.

Serve:
- Serve the Garlic Butter Shrimp Scampi immediately, and enjoy the wonderful flavors!

This Garlic Butter Shrimp Scampi is a quick and flavorful dish that combines succulent shrimp with a rich and buttery sauce. It's perfect served over pasta for a satisfying meal.

Cajun Shrimp and Sausage Skillet

Ingredients:

- 1 pound large shrimp, peeled and deveined
- 1 pound smoked sausage, sliced into rounds
- 1 tablespoon Cajun seasoning (adjust to taste)
- 1 teaspoon paprika
- 1 teaspoon dried thyme
- 1 teaspoon garlic powder
- 1 teaspoon onion powder
- 1/2 teaspoon cayenne pepper (adjust to taste)
- Salt and black pepper to taste
- 2 tablespoons olive oil
- 1 onion, thinly sliced
- 1 bell pepper, thinly sliced
- 3 cloves garlic, minced
- 1 cup cherry tomatoes, halved
- 1 cup chicken broth
- 2 tablespoons tomato paste
- 2 tablespoons fresh parsley, chopped
- Cooked rice or crusty bread for serving

Instructions:

Season Shrimp and Sausage:
- In a bowl, season the shrimp and sliced sausage with Cajun seasoning, paprika, dried thyme, garlic powder, onion powder, cayenne pepper, salt, and black pepper. Toss to coat evenly.

Sear Shrimp and Sausage:
- Heat olive oil in a large skillet over medium-high heat.
- Add the seasoned shrimp and sausage to the skillet. Sear for about 2-3 minutes per side or until the shrimp turn pink and the sausage gets a nice brown color. Remove from the skillet and set aside.

Sauté Vegetables:
- In the same skillet, add sliced onion and bell pepper. Sauté for 2-3 minutes until softened.

Add Aromatics:
- Add minced garlic to the skillet and sauté for an additional 1 minute until fragrant.

Combine and Deglaze:
- Return the seared shrimp and sausage to the skillet.
- Add cherry tomatoes, chicken broth, and tomato paste. Stir well, scraping up any flavorful bits from the bottom of the skillet.

Simmer:
- Allow the mixture to simmer for 5-7 minutes, letting the flavors meld and the sauce thicken slightly.

Finish and Garnish:
- Sprinkle chopped fresh parsley over the top.

Serve:
- Serve the Cajun Shrimp and Sausage over cooked rice or with crusty bread on the side.

This Cajun Shrimp and Sausage Skillet is a flavorful and hearty dish that brings together the bold flavors of Cajun seasoning, succulent shrimp, and savory sausage. Enjoy the rich and spicy taste over rice or with your favorite bread!

Coconut Curry Shrimp

Ingredients:

- 1 pound large shrimp, peeled and deveined
- 2 tablespoons curry powder
- 1 teaspoon turmeric
- 1 teaspoon cumin
- 1 teaspoon coriander
- 1/2 teaspoon chili powder (adjust to taste)
- 1 tablespoon vegetable oil
- 1 onion, finely chopped
- 3 cloves garlic, minced
- 1 tablespoon fresh ginger, grated
- 1 red bell pepper, thinly sliced
- 1 can (14 ounces) coconut milk
- 1 tablespoon soy sauce
- 1 tablespoon fish sauce
- 1 tablespoon brown sugar
- Juice of 1 lime
- Salt and pepper to taste
- Fresh cilantro for garnish
- Cooked rice for serving

Instructions:

Prepare the Shrimp:
- In a bowl, toss the shrimp with curry powder, turmeric, cumin, coriander, and chili powder. Ensure the shrimp are well-coated with the spices.

Sear the Shrimp:
- Heat vegetable oil in a large skillet over medium-high heat.
- Add the seasoned shrimp to the skillet and cook for 2-3 minutes on each side or until they turn pink and opaque. Remove the shrimp from the skillet and set aside.

Sauté Aromatics:
- In the same skillet, add chopped onion and sauté until softened.

Add Garlic and Ginger:
- Add minced garlic and grated ginger to the skillet. Sauté for an additional 1-2 minutes until fragrant.

Cook Bell Pepper:

- Add sliced red bell pepper to the skillet and cook for another 2-3 minutes until it starts to soften.

Prepare the Coconut Curry Sauce:
- Pour in the coconut milk, soy sauce, fish sauce, and brown sugar. Stir well to combine.

Simmer and Season:
- Allow the sauce to simmer for 5-7 minutes, letting the flavors meld.
- Season with salt and pepper to taste.

Add Shrimp and Lime Juice:
- Return the seared shrimp to the skillet. Squeeze the juice of one lime over the mixture. Stir gently to coat the shrimp in the curry sauce.

Finish and Garnish:
- Garnish with fresh cilantro.

Serve:
- Serve the Coconut Curry Shrimp over cooked rice.

This Coconut Curry Shrimp is a delightful combination of creamy coconut, aromatic spices, and succulent shrimp. It's a quick and flavorful dish that pairs wonderfully with rice for a satisfying meal.

Lemon Garlic Butter Shrimp Skewers

Ingredients:

- 1 pound large shrimp, peeled and deveined
- 3 tablespoons unsalted butter, melted
- 3 cloves garlic, minced
- Zest of 1 lemon
- Juice of 1 lemon
- 1 tablespoon fresh parsley, chopped
- 1/2 teaspoon paprika
- Salt and black pepper to taste
- Wooden skewers, soaked in water

Instructions:

Prepare the Marinade:
- In a bowl, combine melted butter, minced garlic, lemon zest, lemon juice, chopped parsley, paprika, salt, and black pepper. Mix well to create the marinade.

Marinate the Shrimp:
- Place the peeled and deveined shrimp in a shallow dish.
- Pour the marinade over the shrimp, ensuring they are well-coated. Allow them to marinate for at least 15-30 minutes in the refrigerator.

Preheat the Grill or Broiler:
- Preheat your grill or broiler to medium-high heat.

Skewer the Shrimp:
- Thread the marinated shrimp onto the soaked wooden skewers, making sure they are secure but not overcrowded.

Grill or Broil the Shrimp:
- If using a grill, place the shrimp skewers directly on the grates. Grill for 2-3 minutes per side or until the shrimp are opaque and have grill marks.
- If using a broiler, place the skewers on a broiler pan and broil for 2-3 minutes per side, keeping a close eye to prevent burning.

Baste with Marinade:
- During grilling or broiling, baste the shrimp with the remaining marinade for added flavor.

Serve:
- Carefully remove the shrimp skewers from the grill or broiler.

Garnish and Enjoy:

- Garnish with additional chopped parsley.
- Serve the Lemon Garlic Butter Shrimp Skewers with your favorite side dishes or over a bed of rice.

These shrimp skewers are bursting with the flavors of lemon, garlic, and butter. They make for a quick and tasty dish, perfect for a light meal or as a flavorful appetizer.

Honey Sriracha Shrimp Stir-Fry

Ingredients:

For the Stir-Fry Sauce:

- 3 tablespoons soy sauce
- 2 tablespoons honey
- 1 tablespoon Sriracha sauce (adjust to taste)
- 1 tablespoon rice vinegar
- 1 teaspoon sesame oil

For the Stir-Fry:

- 1 pound large shrimp, peeled and deveined
- 2 tablespoons vegetable oil
- 3 cloves garlic, minced
- 1 tablespoon fresh ginger, grated
- 1 bell pepper, thinly sliced
- 1 cup snap peas, ends trimmed
- 1 carrot, julienned
- 4 green onions, sliced
- Sesame seeds for garnish
- Cooked rice or noodles for serving

Instructions:

Prepare the Stir-Fry Sauce:

Combine Ingredients:
- In a bowl, whisk together soy sauce, honey, Sriracha sauce, rice vinegar, and sesame oil. Set aside.

Prepare the Stir-Fry:

Marinate Shrimp:
- Place the peeled and deveined shrimp in a bowl.
- Pour a small amount of the prepared stir-fry sauce over the shrimp and toss to coat. Let it marinate for about 10 minutes.

Heat Oil:
- Heat vegetable oil in a wok or large skillet over medium-high heat.

Sauté Garlic and Ginger:
- Add minced garlic and grated ginger to the hot oil. Sauté for about 30 seconds until fragrant.

Cook Shrimp:
- Add the marinated shrimp to the wok. Cook for 2-3 minutes until they start to turn pink.

Add Vegetables:
- Add sliced bell pepper, snap peas, julienned carrot, and sliced green onions to the wok. Stir-fry for an additional 3-4 minutes until the vegetables are tender-crisp.

Pour in Sauce:
- Pour the remaining stir-fry sauce over the shrimp and vegetables. Toss to coat evenly.

Finish and Garnish:
- Continue to stir-fry for an additional 1-2 minutes until everything is well-coated and heated through.
- Garnish with sesame seeds.

Serve:
- Serve the Honey Sriracha Shrimp Stir-Fry over cooked rice or noodles.

This stir-fry combines the sweetness of honey with the heat of Sriracha, creating a perfect balance of flavors. It's a quick and delicious dish that's sure to satisfy your taste buds.

Grilled Chimichurri Shrimp

Ingredients:

For the Chimichurri Sauce:

- 1 cup fresh parsley, chopped
- 1/4 cup fresh cilantro, chopped
- 4 cloves garlic, minced
- 1/2 cup extra-virgin olive oil
- 1/4 cup red wine vinegar
- 1 teaspoon dried oregano
- 1/2 teaspoon red pepper flakes (adjust to taste)
- Salt and black pepper to taste

For the Grilled Shrimp:

- 1 pound large shrimp, peeled and deveined
- 2 tablespoons olive oil
- Juice of 1 lemon
- Salt and black pepper to taste
- Wooden skewers, soaked in water

Instructions:

Prepare the Chimichurri Sauce:

Combine Ingredients:
- In a bowl, mix together chopped parsley, chopped cilantro, minced garlic, olive oil, red wine vinegar, dried oregano, red pepper flakes, salt, and black pepper. Stir well to combine.

Prepare and Grill the Shrimp:

Marinate Shrimp:
- Place the peeled and deveined shrimp in a bowl.
- Drizzle olive oil and lemon juice over the shrimp. Season with salt and black pepper. Toss to coat evenly and let it marinate for about 15-30 minutes.

Skewer the Shrimp:
- Thread the marinated shrimp onto the soaked wooden skewers.

Preheat the Grill:
- Preheat your grill to medium-high heat.

Grill the Shrimp:
- Place the shrimp skewers on the preheated grill.
- Grill for about 2-3 minutes per side or until the shrimp are opaque and have grill marks.

Serve with Chimichurri:
- Remove the shrimp skewers from the grill.
- Drizzle the chimichurri sauce over the grilled shrimp or serve it on the side.

Garnish and Enjoy:
- Garnish with additional fresh herbs if desired.
- Serve the Grilled Chimichurri Shrimp as an appetizer or as part of a main course with your favorite sides.

This recipe brings together the bold flavors of chimichurri with succulent grilled shrimp, creating a delicious and vibrant dish. It's perfect for a barbecue or any outdoor gathering.

Shrimp and Broccoli Alfredo

Ingredients:

- 8 ounces fettuccine pasta
- 1 pound large shrimp, peeled and deveined
- Salt and black pepper to taste
- 2 tablespoons olive oil
- 3 cloves garlic, minced
- 1 cup broccoli florets, blanched
- 1 cup heavy cream
- 1/2 cup unsalted butter
- 1 cup grated Parmesan cheese
- 1 teaspoon garlic powder
- 1 teaspoon onion powder
- 1/2 teaspoon nutmeg (optional)
- Fresh parsley for garnish

Instructions:

Cook the Pasta:
- Cook the fettuccine pasta according to the package instructions until al dente. Drain and set aside.

Prepare the Shrimp:
- Season the peeled and deveined shrimp with salt and black pepper.
- In a large skillet, heat olive oil over medium-high heat.
- Add minced garlic and sauté for about 30 seconds until fragrant.
- Add the seasoned shrimp and cook for 2-3 minutes per side until they turn pink and opaque. Remove the shrimp from the skillet and set aside.

Blanch Broccoli:
- In the same skillet, blanch the broccoli florets in boiling water for 1-2 minutes until they are slightly tender. Drain and set aside.

Prepare the Alfredo Sauce:
- In the skillet, melt unsalted butter over medium heat.
- Pour in the heavy cream and bring it to a gentle simmer.
- Add grated Parmesan cheese, garlic powder, onion powder, and nutmeg (if using). Stir continuously until the cheese is melted and the sauce has thickened.

Combine Ingredients:

- Add the cooked fettuccine pasta, blanched broccoli, and cooked shrimp to the Alfredo sauce. Toss everything together until well coated.

Adjust Seasoning:
- Taste and adjust the seasoning with salt and black pepper if needed.

Garnish and Serve:
- Garnish with fresh parsley.
- Serve the Shrimp and Broccoli Alfredo immediately.

This Shrimp and Broccoli Alfredo is a comforting and flavorful pasta dish that combines succulent shrimp, tender broccoli, and a creamy Alfredo sauce. It's perfect for a satisfying meal that comes together quickly.

Bang Bang Shrimp Tacos

Ingredients:

For the Bang Bang Sauce:

- 1/2 cup mayonnaise
- 3 tablespoons sweet chili sauce
- 1 tablespoon Sriracha sauce
- 1 tablespoon honey
- 1 teaspoon rice vinegar

For the Bang Bang Shrimp:

- 1 pound large shrimp, peeled and deveined
- 1 cup buttermilk
- 1 cup all-purpose flour
- 1 cup panko breadcrumbs
- 1 teaspoon garlic powder
- 1 teaspoon onion powder
- Salt and black pepper to taste
- Vegetable oil for frying

For the Tacos:

- Soft taco shells or tortillas
- Shredded lettuce
- Diced tomatoes
- Sliced green onions
- Cilantro leaves for garnish
- Lime wedges for serving

Instructions:

Prepare the Bang Bang Sauce:

Whisk Ingredients:
- In a bowl, whisk together mayonnaise, sweet chili sauce, Sriracha sauce, honey, and rice vinegar. Set aside.

Prepare the Bang Bang Shrimp:

Marinate Shrimp:
- Place peeled and deveined shrimp in a bowl and pour buttermilk over them. Let them marinate for at least 15-30 minutes.

Prepare Breading:
- In a separate bowl, combine flour, panko breadcrumbs, garlic powder, onion powder, salt, and black pepper.

Bread the Shrimp:
- Remove each shrimp from the buttermilk and dredge it in the flour mixture, ensuring it is evenly coated. Set breaded shrimp aside.

Fry the Shrimp:
- In a large skillet, heat vegetable oil over medium-high heat.
- Fry the breaded shrimp for about 2-3 minutes per side or until they are golden brown and cooked through. Drain on paper towels.

Assemble the Tacos:

Prepare Tacos:
- Warm the soft taco shells or tortillas according to package instructions.

Assemble Tacos:
- Place shredded lettuce on each taco shell.
- Add a few pieces of the crispy Bang Bang Shrimp on top.
- Drizzle the Bang Bang Sauce over the shrimp.
- Top with diced tomatoes, sliced green onions, and cilantro leaves.

Serve:
- Serve the Bang Bang Shrimp Tacos with lime wedges on the side.

These Bang Bang Shrimp Tacos are a delightful combination of crispy shrimp coated in a flavorful sauce, paired with fresh and crunchy taco toppings. They make for a delicious and visually appealing meal that's perfect for any occasion.

Garlic Parmesan Baked Shrimp

Ingredients:

- 1 pound large shrimp, peeled and deveined
- 3 tablespoons melted butter
- 4 cloves garlic, minced
- 1/4 cup grated Parmesan cheese
- 1/4 cup breadcrumbs (Panko or regular)
- 1 tablespoon fresh parsley, chopped
- 1 teaspoon lemon juice
- Salt and black pepper to taste
- Lemon wedges for serving

Instructions:

Preheat the Oven:
- Preheat your oven to 425°F (220°C). Grease a baking dish with cooking spray or a small amount of butter.

Prepare the Shrimp:
- Pat the peeled and deveined shrimp dry with paper towels.
- In a bowl, toss the shrimp with melted butter, minced garlic, grated Parmesan cheese, breadcrumbs, chopped parsley, lemon juice, salt, and black pepper. Ensure the shrimp are evenly coated.

Arrange in Baking Dish:
- Place the coated shrimp in a single layer in the prepared baking dish.

Bake in the Oven:
- Bake the shrimp in the preheated oven for about 12-15 minutes or until they are cooked through and the topping is golden brown.

Broil (Optional):
- If you want to achieve a more golden and crispy top, you can broil the shrimp for an additional 1-2 minutes, keeping a close eye to prevent burning.

Serve:
- Carefully remove the baked shrimp from the oven.

Garnish and Enjoy:
- Garnish with additional chopped parsley.
- Serve the Garlic Parmesan Baked Shrimp with lemon wedges on the side.

These Garlic Parmesan Baked Shrimp are wonderfully flavorful and make for a quick and easy dish. The combination of garlic, Parmesan, and breadcrumbs creates a crispy and savory coating that complements the succulent shrimp. Enjoy them as an appetizer or as part of a seafood dinner!

Spicy Thai Shrimp Salad

Ingredients:

For the Shrimp:

- 1 pound large shrimp, peeled and deveined
- 1 tablespoon soy sauce
- 1 tablespoon fish sauce
- 1 tablespoon Sriracha sauce (adjust to taste)
- 1 tablespoon vegetable oil

For the Salad:

- 4 cups mixed salad greens (lettuce, spinach, arugula, etc.)
- 1 cucumber, thinly sliced
- 1 carrot, julienned
- 1 bell pepper, thinly sliced
- 1/2 red onion, thinly sliced
- 1/4 cup fresh cilantro, chopped
- 1/4 cup fresh mint leaves, chopped
- 1/4 cup roasted peanuts, chopped

For the Dressing:

- 3 tablespoons lime juice
- 2 tablespoons fish sauce
- 1 tablespoon soy sauce
- 1 tablespoon brown sugar
- 1 tablespoon Sriracha sauce
- 2 cloves garlic, minced
- 1 tablespoon ginger, grated

Instructions:

Prepare the Shrimp:

    Marinate Shrimp:
- In a bowl, combine soy sauce, fish sauce, Sriracha sauce, and vegetable oil. Add the peeled and deveined shrimp, tossing to coat. Let it marinate for 15-30 minutes.

    Cook Shrimp:
- Heat a skillet or grill pan over medium-high heat.

- Cook the marinated shrimp for 2-3 minutes per side or until they are pink and opaque. Set aside.

Prepare the Salad:

Assemble Salad:
- In a large salad bowl, combine mixed greens, sliced cucumber, julienned carrot, sliced bell pepper, sliced red onion, chopped cilantro, and chopped mint.

Prepare the Dressing:

Whisk Dressing:
- In a small bowl, whisk together lime juice, fish sauce, soy sauce, brown sugar, Sriracha sauce, minced garlic, and grated ginger.

Assemble and Serve:

Combine Shrimp and Salad:
- Add the cooked shrimp to the salad.

Drizzle Dressing:
- Drizzle the dressing over the salad and shrimp. Toss everything together to coat evenly.

Garnish and Serve:
- Garnish the salad with chopped roasted peanuts.
- Serve the Spicy Thai Shrimp Salad immediately.

This Spicy Thai Shrimp Salad is a refreshing and vibrant dish that combines the bold flavors of Thai cuisine. The combination of spicy shrimp, crisp vegetables, and the zesty dressing makes it a perfect light and satisfying meal. Enjoy!

Scallop Recipes:

Pan-Seared Scallops with White Wine Sauce

Ingredients:

For the Scallops:

- 1 pound large sea scallops, side muscle removed
- Salt and black pepper to taste
- 2 tablespoons olive oil
- 2 tablespoons unsalted butter
- Fresh parsley for garnish

For the White Wine Sauce:

- 1/2 cup dry white wine
- 1/4 cup chicken or seafood broth
- 2 tablespoons shallots, finely chopped
- 2 cloves garlic, minced
- 2 tablespoons heavy cream
- 1 tablespoon fresh lemon juice
- 1 tablespoon fresh parsley, chopped
- Salt and black pepper to taste

Instructions:

Prepare the Scallops:

    Dry the Scallops:
- Pat the scallops dry with paper towels to remove excess moisture. Season them with salt and black pepper.

    Preheat the Pan:
- Heat a large skillet or frying pan over medium-high heat.

    Sear the Scallops:
- Add olive oil and 1 tablespoon of butter to the hot pan.
- Place the scallops in the pan, making sure not to overcrowd them. Sear for 2-3 minutes on each side until they develop a golden brown crust. Do not overcook; scallops should be opaque in the center.

    Remove from Pan:
- Once the scallops are cooked, remove them from the pan and set aside.

Prepare the White Wine Sauce:

Sauté Shallots and Garlic:
- In the same pan, add chopped shallots and minced garlic. Sauté for about 1-2 minutes until they become translucent.

Deglaze with White Wine:
- Pour in the white wine, using a spatula to scrape up any flavorful bits from the bottom of the pan. Allow the wine to reduce for a couple of minutes.

Add Broth and Cream:
- Add chicken or seafood broth to the pan and stir.
- Stir in the heavy cream and let the mixture simmer for another 2-3 minutes.

Season and Finish:
- Season the sauce with salt and black pepper to taste.
- Stir in fresh lemon juice and chopped parsley.

Serve:

Plate the Scallops:
- Arrange the pan-seared scallops on serving plates.

Pour Sauce Over Scallops:
- Pour the white wine sauce over the scallops.

Garnish and Enjoy:
- Garnish with fresh parsley.
- Serve the Pan-Seared Scallops with White Wine Sauce immediately.

This elegant dish of Pan-Seared Scallops with White Wine Sauce is perfect for a special occasion or a luxurious dinner at home. The combination of perfectly seared scallops with a flavorful white wine sauce creates a delightful and sophisticated meal. Enjoy!

Bacon-Wrapped Scallops

Ingredients:

- 1 pound large sea scallops, side muscle removed
- 10-12 slices of bacon, cut in half
- Salt and black pepper to taste
- 1 tablespoon olive oil
- Toothpicks

Instructions:

Preheat the Oven:
- Preheat your oven to 400°F (200°C).

Prepare the Scallops:
- Pat the scallops dry with paper towels to remove excess moisture.
- Season the scallops with salt and black pepper to taste.

Wrap Scallops with Bacon:
- Take a half-slice of bacon and wrap it around each scallop, securing it with a toothpick. Repeat for all the scallops.

Preheat a Skillet:
- Heat olive oil in an oven-safe skillet over medium-high heat.

Sear the Bacon-Wrapped Scallops:
- Place the bacon-wrapped scallops in the skillet and sear for about 1-2 minutes on each side, just until the bacon starts to crisp up.

Transfer to the Oven:
- Transfer the skillet to the preheated oven.

Bake:
- Bake the bacon-wrapped scallops in the oven for approximately 10-15 minutes or until the bacon is crispy and the scallops are cooked through.

Broil (Optional):
- If you want the bacon to be extra crispy, you can broil the scallops for an additional 1-2 minutes, keeping a close eye to prevent burning.

Serve:
- Carefully remove the skillet from the oven.
- Serve the Bacon-Wrapped Scallops immediately, removing the toothpicks before serving.

Enjoy these Bacon-Wrapped Scallops as an appetizer or as part of a seafood-themed meal. The combination of succulent scallops and crispy bacon is sure to be a crowd-pleaser!

Lemon Garlic Butter Scallops

Ingredients:

- 1 pound large sea scallops, side muscle removed
- Salt and black pepper to taste
- 2 tablespoons olive oil
- 3 tablespoons unsalted butter
- 4 cloves garlic, minced
- Zest of 1 lemon
- Juice of 1 lemon
- 2 tablespoons fresh parsley, chopped
- Lemon wedges for serving

Instructions:

Prepare the Scallops:
- Pat the scallops dry with paper towels to remove excess moisture.
- Season the scallops with salt and black pepper to taste.

Preheat a Skillet:
- Heat olive oil in a large skillet over medium-high heat.

Sear the Scallops:
- Place the scallops in the skillet, making sure not to overcrowd them. Sear for 1-2 minutes on each side until they develop a golden brown crust. Be careful not to overcook; scallops should be opaque in the center.

Add Butter and Garlic:
- Add unsalted butter to the skillet. Once melted, add minced garlic and sauté for about 1 minute until the garlic becomes fragrant.

Add Lemon Zest and Juice:
- Stir in the lemon zest and lemon juice. Toss the scallops in the lemon garlic butter sauce to coat them evenly.

Finish with Parsley:
- Sprinkle chopped fresh parsley over the scallops. Toss once more to incorporate.

Serve:
- Transfer the Lemon Garlic Butter Scallops to a serving plate.
- Serve immediately, with lemon wedges on the side.

These Lemon Garlic Butter Scallops are a simple yet elegant dish that highlights the natural sweetness of the scallops. The combination of garlic, butter, and lemon adds a burst of flavor that complements the delicate taste of the seafood. Enjoy this dish as a main course or a delightful appetizer!

Scallop and Asparagus Risotto

Ingredients:

- 1 pound large sea scallops, side muscle removed
- 1 cup Arborio rice
- 1/2 cup dry white wine
- 4 cups chicken or vegetable broth, kept warm
- 1 cup asparagus spears, trimmed and cut into bite-sized pieces
- 1/2 cup grated Parmesan cheese
- 1 small onion, finely chopped
- 2 cloves garlic, minced
- 2 tablespoons olive oil
- 2 tablespoons unsalted butter
- Salt and black pepper to taste
- Fresh parsley for garnish
- Lemon wedges for serving

Instructions:

Prepare the Asparagus:
- Blanch the asparagus pieces in boiling water for 2-3 minutes until they are slightly tender. Drain and set aside.

Sear the Scallops:
- Pat the scallops dry with paper towels. Season with salt and black pepper.
- In a skillet over medium-high heat, add 1 tablespoon of olive oil. Sear the scallops for 1-2 minutes on each side until they develop a golden brown crust. Remove from the skillet and set aside.

Start the Risotto:
- In the same skillet, add 1 tablespoon of olive oil and 1 tablespoon of butter. Sauté the chopped onion and minced garlic until they become translucent.

Cook the Rice:
- Add Arborio rice to the skillet and cook for 1-2 minutes, stirring constantly, until the rice is well-coated and slightly toasted.

Deglaze with Wine:
- Pour in the dry white wine and stir until it's mostly absorbed by the rice.

Add Broth:

- Begin adding the warm chicken or vegetable broth one ladle at a time. Allow the liquid to be absorbed before adding the next ladle. Stir frequently.

Incorporate Asparagus:
- When the rice is nearly cooked (after about 15-18 minutes), stir in the blanched asparagus pieces.

Finish the Risotto:
- Continue adding broth and stirring until the rice is creamy and cooked to al dente. This process may take around 20-25 minutes.

Add Parmesan Cheese:
- Stir in the grated Parmesan cheese to create a creamy texture.

Season and Serve:
- Season the risotto with salt and black pepper to taste.
- Plate the risotto and top with the seared scallops.

Garnish and Enjoy:
- Garnish with fresh parsley.
- Serve the Scallop and Asparagus Risotto immediately, with lemon wedges on the side.

This Scallop and Asparagus Risotto is a luxurious and comforting dish that combines the richness of sea scallops with the vibrant flavors of asparagus in a creamy risotto. Enjoy this restaurant-worthy meal at home!

Coconut Curry Scallop Stir-Fry

Ingredients:

For the Coconut Curry Sauce:

- 1 can (14 ounces) coconut milk
- 2 tablespoons red curry paste
- 1 tablespoon soy sauce
- 1 tablespoon fish sauce
- 1 tablespoon brown sugar
- 1 tablespoon lime juice

For the Stir-Fry:

- 1 pound large sea scallops, side muscle removed
- 2 tablespoons vegetable oil
- 1 bell pepper, thinly sliced
- 1 zucchini, thinly sliced
- 1 carrot, julienned
- 1 cup snap peas, ends trimmed
- 3 cloves garlic, minced
- 1 tablespoon fresh ginger, grated
- Cooked jasmine rice or rice noodles for serving
- Fresh cilantro for garnish
- Lime wedges for serving

Instructions:

Prepare the Coconut Curry Sauce:

Mix Ingredients:
- In a bowl, whisk together coconut milk, red curry paste, soy sauce, fish sauce, brown sugar, and lime juice. Set aside.

Prepare the Scallop Stir-Fry:

Prepare Scallops:
- Pat the scallops dry with paper towels. Season them with salt and black pepper.

Sear Scallops:

- Heat vegetable oil in a wok or large skillet over medium-high heat.
- Sear the scallops for 1-2 minutes on each side until they develop a golden brown crust. Remove from the wok and set aside.

Sauté Vegetables:
- In the same wok, add a bit more oil if needed. Sauté sliced bell pepper, zucchini, julienned carrot, and snap peas until they are crisp-tender.

Add Garlic and Ginger:
- Add minced garlic and grated ginger to the vegetables. Sauté for an additional 1-2 minutes until fragrant.

Combine with Sauce:
- Pour the prepared coconut curry sauce into the wok. Stir well to combine with the vegetables.

Add Scallops:
- Gently add the seared scallops back to the wok. Allow them to simmer in the sauce for 2-3 minutes to absorb the flavors.

Serve:
- Serve the Coconut Curry Scallop Stir-Fry over cooked jasmine rice or rice noodles.

Garnish and Enjoy:
- Garnish with fresh cilantro and serve with lime wedges on the side.

This Coconut Curry Scallop Stir-Fry is a delightful combination of succulent scallops, crisp vegetables, and a creamy coconut curry sauce. It's a quick and flavorful dish that pairs perfectly with jasmine rice or rice noodles. Enjoy!

Herb-Crusted Baked Scallops

Ingredients:

For the Herb Crust:

- 1 cup fresh breadcrumbs
- 1/4 cup fresh parsley, chopped
- 2 tablespoons fresh chives, chopped
- 1 tablespoon fresh thyme leaves
- 2 cloves garlic, minced
- Zest of 1 lemon
- 2 tablespoons Parmesan cheese, grated
- Salt and black pepper to taste
- 3 tablespoons olive oil

For the Scallops:

- 1 pound large sea scallops, side muscle removed
- 2 tablespoons unsalted butter, melted
- 1 tablespoon lemon juice
- Salt and black pepper to taste

Instructions:

Prepare the Herb Crust:

  Preheat Oven:
  - Preheat your oven to 425°F (220°C).

  Make Herb Crust:
  - In a bowl, combine fresh breadcrumbs, chopped parsley, chopped chives, thyme leaves, minced garlic, lemon zest, Parmesan cheese, salt, and black pepper.
  - Drizzle olive oil over the mixture and toss to combine until the breadcrumbs are coated evenly.

Prepare the Scallops:

  Season Scallops:
  - Pat the scallops dry with paper towels.

- In a separate bowl, mix melted butter and lemon juice. Season the scallops with salt and black pepper, then toss them in the butter and lemon mixture.

Coat Scallops with Herb Crust:
- Roll each seasoned scallop in the herb crust mixture, ensuring they are coated thoroughly.

Bake:
- Place the herb-crusted scallops on a baking sheet lined with parchment paper or a greased baking dish.

Bake in the Oven:
- Bake in the preheated oven for about 12-15 minutes or until the scallops are cooked through and the crust is golden brown.

Broil (Optional):
- For an extra crispiness, you can broil the scallops for an additional 1-2 minutes, keeping a close eye to prevent burning.

Serve:
- Carefully remove the baked scallops from the oven.

Garnish and Enjoy:
- Garnish with additional fresh herbs if desired.
- Serve the Herb-Crusted Baked Scallops immediately.

These Herb-Crusted Baked Scallops are a delightful combination of tender scallops with a flavorful and crunchy herb crust. Enjoy them as an elegant appetizer or as part of a seafood dinner!

Scallop and Corn Chowder

Ingredients:

- 1 pound large sea scallops, side muscle removed and halved
- 4 slices bacon, chopped
- 1 large onion, diced
- 2 cloves garlic, minced
- 2 carrots, diced
- 2 celery stalks, diced
- 3 potatoes, peeled and diced
- 1 red bell pepper, diced
- 1 cup corn kernels (fresh or frozen)
- 4 cups chicken or vegetable broth
- 1 cup whole milk or half-and-half
- 2 tablespoons all-purpose flour
- 2 tablespoons unsalted butter
- 1 bay leaf
- 1 teaspoon dried thyme
- Salt and black pepper to taste
- Fresh parsley for garnish

Instructions:

Cook Bacon:
- In a large soup pot or Dutch oven, cook the chopped bacon over medium heat until crispy. Remove the bacon with a slotted spoon and set aside for garnish.

Sauté Vegetables:
- In the same pot, add diced onion, minced garlic, carrots, celery, and red bell pepper. Sauté for 5-7 minutes until the vegetables are softened.

Add Potatoes and Corn:
- Stir in diced potatoes and corn kernels, and continue to cook for another 3-4 minutes.

Make Roux:
- Melt butter in the pot, then sprinkle flour over the vegetables. Stir well to create a roux.

Pour Broth and Milk:
- Gradually pour in the chicken or vegetable broth while stirring to avoid lumps.

- Add whole milk or half-and-half, bay leaf, and dried thyme. Season with salt and black pepper to taste.

Simmer Chowder:
- Bring the chowder to a simmer and let it cook for about 15-20 minutes until the potatoes are tender.

Cook Scallops:
- While the chowder simmers, season the halved scallops with salt and pepper.
- In a separate skillet, sear the scallops over medium-high heat for 1-2 minutes per side until they develop a golden crust. Remove from the skillet and set aside.

Finish Chowder:
- Once the potatoes are tender, discard the bay leaf.
- Gently stir in the seared scallops and let them warm through for 2-3 minutes.

Serve:
- Ladle the Scallop and Corn Chowder into bowls.
- Garnish with crispy bacon and fresh parsley.

Enjoy:
- Serve the chowder hot and enjoy your delicious Scallop and Corn Chowder!

This chowder is a hearty and satisfying dish that combines the sweetness of scallops with the rich flavors of bacon and corn. It's perfect for warming up on a chilly day!

Grilled Scallop and Mango Skewers

Ingredients:

For the Marinade:

- 1 pound large sea scallops, side muscle removed
- 2 tablespoons olive oil
- 2 tablespoons lime juice
- 2 cloves garlic, minced
- 1 teaspoon honey
- 1 teaspoon ground cumin
- 1 teaspoon paprika
- Salt and black pepper to taste

For the Skewers:

- 2 ripe mangoes, peeled and cut into chunks
- Red onion, cut into chunks (optional)
- Bell peppers (red, yellow, or green), cut into chunks
- Wooden skewers, soaked in water for 30 minutes

For Garnish:

- Fresh cilantro, chopped
- Lime wedges for serving

Instructions:

Prepare Marinade:
- In a bowl, whisk together olive oil, lime juice, minced garlic, honey, ground cumin, paprika, salt, and black pepper.

Marinate Scallops:
- Place the sea scallops in a shallow dish and pour the marinade over them. Toss to coat the scallops evenly. Let them marinate for about 15-30 minutes.

Preheat Grill:
- Preheat your grill to medium-high heat.

Assemble Skewers:
- Thread the marinated scallops, mango chunks, red onion (if using), and bell peppers onto the soaked wooden skewers, alternating as desired.

Grill Skewers:
- Place the skewers on the preheated grill and cook for about 2-3 minutes per side or until the scallops are opaque and have grill marks.

Baste with Marinade:
- Occasionally baste the skewers with the remaining marinade during grilling.

Remove from Grill:
- Once the scallops are cooked and the skewers have a nice char, remove them from the grill.

Garnish and Serve:
- Sprinkle chopped fresh cilantro over the grilled scallop and mango skewers.
- Serve the skewers with lime wedges on the side.

These Grilled Scallop and Mango Skewers are a delightful combination of sweet and savory flavors, making them perfect for a summer barbecue or a light and refreshing meal. Enjoy!

Scallops with Brown Butter and Sage

Ingredients:

- 1 pound large sea scallops, side muscle removed
- Salt and black pepper to taste
- 2 tablespoons olive oil
- 4 tablespoons unsalted butter
- Fresh sage leaves
- 1 tablespoon lemon juice (optional)
- Lemon wedges for serving

Instructions:

Pat Dry Scallops:
- Pat the scallops dry with paper towels to remove excess moisture. Season them with salt and black pepper.

Preheat Skillet:
- Heat olive oil in a large skillet over medium-high heat.

Sear Scallops:
- Once the skillet is hot, add the scallops. Sear for 1-2 minutes on each side until they develop a golden brown crust. Be careful not to overcook; scallops should be opaque in the center.

Brown Butter and Sage:
- Add unsalted butter to the skillet. Allow it to melt and continue cooking until it turns golden brown. Add fresh sage leaves to the browned butter and let them crisp up for about 1-2 minutes.

Baste Scallops:
- Tilt the skillet slightly and use a spoon to baste the scallops with the brown butter and sage mixture. This adds flavor to the scallops.

Finish with Lemon Juice:
- Optionally, squeeze lemon juice over the scallops for a citrusy kick. Stir gently to combine.

Serve:
- Transfer the scallops to a serving plate.
- Pour the brown butter and sage sauce over the scallops.

Garnish and Enjoy:
- Garnish with additional fresh sage leaves.
- Serve the Scallops with Brown Butter and Sage immediately, with lemon wedges on the side.

This dish of Scallops with Brown Butter and Sage is a classic and elegant preparation that highlights the sweet flavor of the scallops with the rich and nutty taste of brown butter. Enjoy this quick and flavorful seafood delight!

Scallop and Avocado Ceviche

Ingredients:

For the Ceviche:

- 1/2 pound fresh sea scallops, thinly sliced
- 1/2 cup fresh lime juice
- 1/2 cup fresh lemon juice
- 1/2 red onion, finely diced
- 1 jalapeño pepper, seeds removed and finely chopped
- 1 cup cherry tomatoes, halved
- 1/2 cup cucumber, diced
- 1/4 cup fresh cilantro, chopped
- Salt and black pepper to taste

For Serving:

- 2 ripe avocados, diced
- Tortilla chips or tostadas

Instructions:

Prepare the Scallops:
- In a bowl, combine the thinly sliced scallops with lime juice and lemon juice. Ensure the scallops are fully submerged in the citrus juice. Let them marinate for about 20-30 minutes, or until the scallops turn opaque.

Combine Ingredients:
- Drain the excess citrus juice from the scallops.
- In a large bowl, combine the marinated scallops with finely diced red onion, chopped jalapeño, halved cherry tomatoes, diced cucumber, and chopped cilantro.

Season the Ceviche:
- Season the ceviche with salt and black pepper to taste. Mix everything well to ensure even distribution of flavors.

Chill:
- Cover the bowl with plastic wrap and refrigerate the ceviche for at least 1 hour to allow the flavors to meld.

Prepare Avocado:
- Just before serving, gently fold in the diced avocados.

Serve:

- Serve the Scallop and Avocado Ceviche in bowls or on tostadas.

Garnish and Enjoy:
- Garnish with additional cilantro if desired.
- Serve with tortilla chips or tostadas on the side.

This Scallop and Avocado Ceviche is a light and refreshing dish that showcases the delicate flavor of scallops combined with the creaminess of ripe avocados. It makes for a perfect appetizer or light meal, especially on warm days. Enjoy!

Crab Recipes:
Crab Stuffed Mushrooms

Ingredients:

- 1 pound large mushrooms, cleaned and stems removed
- 8 ounces lump crabmeat, drained and picked over for shells
- 1/2 cup cream cheese, softened
- 1/4 cup mayonnaise
- 1/4 cup grated Parmesan cheese
- 2 green onions, finely chopped
- 2 cloves garlic, minced
- 1 teaspoon Dijon mustard
- 1 teaspoon Worcestershire sauce
- 1/2 teaspoon Old Bay seasoning (optional)
- Salt and black pepper to taste
- 1/4 cup breadcrumbs (Panko or regular)
- Fresh parsley, chopped, for garnish

Instructions:

Preheat Oven:
- Preheat your oven to 375°F (190°C).

Prepare Mushrooms:
- Clean the mushrooms and remove the stems. Place the mushroom caps on a baking sheet.

Prepare Crab Mixture:
- In a mixing bowl, combine lump crabmeat, cream cheese, mayonnaise, grated Parmesan cheese, green onions, minced garlic, Dijon mustard, Worcestershire sauce, Old Bay seasoning (if using), salt, and black pepper. Mix until well combined.

Stuff the Mushrooms:
- Spoon the crab mixture into each mushroom cap, pressing down slightly to ensure it's packed.

Top with Breadcrumbs:
- Sprinkle breadcrumbs over the stuffed mushrooms. This adds a crunchy texture.

Bake:

- Bake in the preheated oven for about 15-20 minutes or until the mushrooms are tender, and the tops are golden brown.

Garnish:
- Remove from the oven and garnish with chopped fresh parsley.

Serve:
- Serve the Crab Stuffed Mushrooms hot.

These Crab Stuffed Mushrooms make for an elegant and flavorful appetizer, perfect for parties or special occasions. The combination of creamy crab filling and the earthy flavor of mushrooms is sure to be a crowd-pleaser. Enjoy!

Creamy Crab and Spinach Dip

Ingredients:

- 8 ounces lump crabmeat, drained and picked over for shells
- 1 cup fresh spinach, chopped
- 1/2 cup mayonnaise
- 1/2 cup sour cream
- 1 cup cream cheese, softened
- 1 cup shredded mozzarella cheese
- 1/2 cup grated Parmesan cheese
- 1/4 cup chopped green onions
- 2 cloves garlic, minced
- 1 tablespoon lemon juice
- 1 teaspoon Worcestershire sauce
- 1/2 teaspoon hot sauce (optional)
- Salt and black pepper to taste
- 1 tablespoon olive oil (for greasing baking dish)
- Baguette slices, tortilla chips, or vegetable sticks for serving

Instructions:

Preheat Oven:
- Preheat your oven to 375°F (190°C).

Prepare Crab and Spinach:
- In a large mixing bowl, combine lump crabmeat and chopped fresh spinach.

Prepare Creamy Base:
- In a separate bowl, mix together mayonnaise, sour cream, softened cream cheese, shredded mozzarella, grated Parmesan, chopped green onions, minced garlic, lemon juice, Worcestershire sauce, hot sauce (if using), salt, and black pepper. Stir until well combined.

Combine Crab and Creamy Base:
- Add the creamy mixture to the crab and spinach. Gently fold everything together until evenly combined.

Grease Baking Dish:
- Grease a baking dish with olive oil.

Transfer Mixture to Baking Dish:
- Transfer the creamy crab and spinach mixture to the greased baking dish, spreading it evenly.

Bake:
- Bake in the preheated oven for 25-30 minutes or until the dip is hot and bubbly, and the top is golden brown.

Serve:
- Remove from the oven and let it cool slightly before serving.

Garnish and Enjoy:
- Garnish with additional chopped green onions if desired.
- Serve the Creamy Crab and Spinach Dip with baguette slices, tortilla chips, or vegetable sticks.

This Creamy Crab and Spinach Dip is a crowd-pleasing appetizer with a perfect combination of flavors. It's great for entertaining and is sure to be a hit at any gathering. Enjoy!

Old Bay Crab Cakes

Ingredients:

- 1 pound lump crabmeat, picked over for shells
- 1/3 cup mayonnaise
- 1 large egg, beaten
- 1 tablespoon Dijon mustard
- 1 tablespoon Worcestershire sauce
- 1 teaspoon Old Bay seasoning
- 1 teaspoon lemon juice
- 1/4 cup finely chopped green onions
- 1/4 cup finely chopped parsley
- Salt and black pepper to taste
- 1 cup breadcrumbs (Panko or regular), divided
- Olive oil for frying

Instructions:

Prepare Crab Mixture:
- In a large mixing bowl, combine lump crabmeat, mayonnaise, beaten egg, Dijon mustard, Worcestershire sauce, Old Bay seasoning, lemon juice, chopped green onions, chopped parsley, salt, and black pepper. Gently fold the ingredients together.

Add Breadcrumbs:
- Gradually add 1/2 cup of breadcrumbs to the crab mixture. Mix until the ingredients are well combined.

Shape Crab Cakes:
- Form crab mixture into crab cakes, shaping them into patties. If the mixture is too wet, you can add more breadcrumbs to achieve the desired consistency.

Coat with Breadcrumbs:
- Coat each crab cake with the remaining 1/2 cup of breadcrumbs, pressing the breadcrumbs onto the surface to adhere.

Chill:
- Place the crab cakes on a baking sheet and refrigerate for at least 30 minutes. This helps the crab cakes firm up.

Heat Olive Oil:
- In a skillet, heat olive oil over medium-high heat.

Fry Crab Cakes:

- Fry the crab cakes for about 3-4 minutes per side or until they are golden brown and cooked through.

Drain on Paper Towels:
- Once cooked, transfer the crab cakes to a plate lined with paper towels to drain any excess oil.

Serve:
- Serve the Old Bay Crab Cakes hot.

These Old Bay Crab Cakes are a classic and flavorful dish with the perfect blend of spices. They make a great appetizer or can be served as a main course. Enjoy the delicious taste of the Chesapeake Bay with these delightful crab cakes!

Garlic Butter Roasted Crab Legs

Ingredients:

- 2 pounds crab legs, thawed if frozen
- 1/2 cup unsalted butter, melted
- 4 cloves garlic, minced
- 1 tablespoon fresh parsley, chopped
- 1 tablespoon lemon juice
- 1 teaspoon Old Bay seasoning (optional)
- Salt and black pepper to taste
- Lemon wedges for serving

Instructions:

Preheat Oven:
- Preheat your oven to 400°F (200°C).

Prepare Crab Legs:
- Use kitchen shears to cut the crab legs into manageable pieces, if needed.

Garlic Butter Mixture:
- In a small bowl, mix together melted butter, minced garlic, chopped fresh parsley, lemon juice, Old Bay seasoning (if using), salt, and black pepper.

Coat Crab Legs:
- Place the crab legs on a baking sheet lined with foil or parchment paper.
- Brush the garlic butter mixture generously over the crab legs, ensuring they are well coated.

Roast in the Oven:
- Roast the crab legs in the preheated oven for 12-15 minutes, or until they are heated through.

Baste:
- Occasionally baste the crab legs with the garlic butter mixture while roasting.

Serve:
- Once the crab legs are heated and the garlic butter has caramelized, remove them from the oven.

Garnish and Enjoy:
- Garnish with additional chopped parsley.
- Serve the Garlic Butter Roasted Crab Legs with lemon wedges on the side.

These Garlic Butter Roasted Crab Legs are a simple yet flavorful way to enjoy the sweet and succulent taste of crab. The garlic butter adds richness and enhances the natural flavors of the crab. Serve as a delightful seafood dish for a special occasion or a family dinner. Enjoy!

Crab and Corn Chowder

Ingredients:

- 1 pound lump crabmeat, picked over for shells
- 4 slices bacon, chopped
- 1 onion, finely chopped
- 2 celery stalks, diced
- 2 carrots, diced
- 2 cloves garlic, minced
- 1/4 cup all-purpose flour
- 4 cups chicken broth
- 2 cups fresh or frozen corn kernels
- 1 large potato, peeled and diced
- 1 teaspoon Old Bay seasoning
- 1/2 teaspoon dried thyme
- 1 bay leaf
- 2 cups whole milk
- 1 cup heavy cream
- Salt and black pepper to taste
- Chives or green onions, chopped, for garnish

Instructions:

    Prepare Crab:
- Pick through the lump crabmeat to ensure there are no shells or cartilage. Set aside.

    Cook Bacon:
- In a large soup pot or Dutch oven, cook the chopped bacon over medium heat until it becomes crispy.

    Sauté Vegetables:
- Add finely chopped onion, diced celery, diced carrots, and minced garlic to the pot. Sauté for 5-7 minutes until the vegetables are softened.

    Add Flour:
- Sprinkle all-purpose flour over the vegetables and bacon. Stir well to create a roux, cooking for 2-3 minutes.

    Pour Broth:
- Gradually pour in the chicken broth while stirring to avoid lumps.

    Add Corn, Potato, and Seasonings:

- Add corn kernels, diced potato, Old Bay seasoning, dried thyme, and bay leaf to the pot. Stir to combine.

Simmer:
- Allow the chowder to simmer for about 15-20 minutes until the potatoes are tender.

Add Milk and Cream:
- Pour in the whole milk and heavy cream. Stir well and let the chowder simmer for an additional 5-7 minutes.

Add Crabmeat:
- Gently fold in the lump crabmeat. Be careful not to break up the crabmeat too much.

Season and Garnish:
- Season the chowder with salt and black pepper to taste. Remove the bay leaf.
- Garnish with chopped chives or green onions.

Serve:
- Ladle the Crab and Corn Chowder into bowls.

Enjoy:
- Serve hot and enjoy this comforting and flavorful chowder!

This Crab and Corn Chowder is a rich and hearty soup with the sweetness of corn and the succulence of lump crabmeat. It's perfect for warming up on a chilly day. Enjoy!

Crab Rangoon

Ingredients:

- 8 oz lump crabmeat, drained and picked over for shells
- 8 oz cream cheese, softened
- 2 green onions, finely chopped
- 1 clove garlic, minced
- 1 teaspoon soy sauce
- 1 teaspoon Worcestershire sauce
- 1/2 teaspoon ginger, grated
- 1 package (about 25) wonton wrappers
- Vegetable oil for frying
- Sweet and sour sauce or soy sauce for dipping

Instructions:

Prepare Filling:
- In a mixing bowl, combine lump crabmeat, softened cream cheese, chopped green onions, minced garlic, soy sauce, Worcestershire sauce, and grated ginger. Mix until well combined.

Assemble Crab Rangoon:
- Lay out a wonton wrapper on a clean surface. Place about 1 teaspoon of the crab and cream cheese filling in the center of the wrapper.
- Moisten the edges of the wrapper with a little water.
- Fold the wrapper in half to create a triangle, pressing the edges to seal. Make sure there are no air pockets.
- Optionally, you can fold and pinch the corners together to create a purse-like shape.

Heat Oil:
- In a deep fryer or a large, deep skillet, heat vegetable oil to 350°F (175°C).

Fry Crab Rangoon:
- Carefully add the crab Rangoon to the hot oil, a few at a time. Fry until they turn golden brown, usually about 2-3 minutes per side.
- Use a slotted spoon to remove the fried crab Rangoon and place them on a paper towel-lined plate to absorb any excess oil.

Repeat:
- Repeat the process until all the crab Rangoon are fried.

Serve:

- Serve the Crab Rangoon hot with sweet and sour sauce or soy sauce for dipping.

These Crab Rangoon are crispy on the outside and filled with a creamy and flavorful crab mixture on the inside. They make for a delightful appetizer at parties or a tasty addition to your Chinese takeout night. Enjoy!

Spicy Crab Linguine

Ingredients:

- 8 oz linguine pasta
- 1 pound lump crabmeat, picked over for shells
- 3 tablespoons olive oil
- 4 cloves garlic, minced
- 1 teaspoon red pepper flakes (adjust to taste)
- 1/2 cup cherry tomatoes, halved
- 1/4 cup dry white wine
- Juice of 1 lemon
- 1/4 cup fresh parsley, chopped
- Salt and black pepper to taste
- Grated Parmesan cheese for garnish (optional)

Instructions:

Cook Linguine:
- Cook the linguine pasta according to the package instructions. Drain and set aside.

Prepare Crab:
- Pick through the lump crabmeat to ensure there are no shells or cartilage. Set aside.

Sauté Garlic and Red Pepper Flakes:
- In a large skillet, heat olive oil over medium heat. Add minced garlic and red pepper flakes. Sauté for 1-2 minutes until the garlic becomes fragrant.

Add Tomatoes and Crab:
- Add halved cherry tomatoes to the skillet. Cook for another 2 minutes until the tomatoes begin to soften.
- Gently fold in the lump crabmeat, being careful not to break it up too much. Allow it to heat through.

Deglaze with Wine:
- Pour in the dry white wine to deglaze the skillet. Scrape up any browned bits from the bottom of the pan.

Combine with Pasta:
- Add the cooked linguine to the skillet. Toss everything together to coat the pasta in the crab and tomato mixture.

Season and Finish:

- Squeeze the juice of one lemon over the pasta. Season with salt and black pepper to taste. Toss again to combine.

Add Fresh Parsley:
- Stir in the chopped fresh parsley for a burst of freshness.

Serve:
- Divide the Spicy Crab Linguine among plates.

Garnish and Enjoy:
- Optionally, garnish with grated Parmesan cheese.
- Serve immediately and enjoy your flavorful and spicy crab linguine!

This Spicy Crab Linguine is a delightful pasta dish that brings together the sweetness of lump crabmeat with a kick of red pepper flakes. It's quick, easy to make, and perfect for a satisfying weeknight dinner or a special occasion. Enjoy!

Avocado and Crab Salad

Ingredients:

For the Salad:

- 1 pound lump crabmeat, picked over for shells
- 2 ripe avocados, diced
- 1 cup cherry tomatoes, halved
- 1 cucumber, diced
- 1/4 cup red onion, finely chopped
- Fresh cilantro or parsley, chopped (for garnish)
- Sesame seeds (optional, for garnish)

For the Dressing:

- 3 tablespoons olive oil
- 2 tablespoons fresh lime juice
- 1 tablespoon soy sauce
- 1 teaspoon honey
- 1 teaspoon Dijon mustard
- 1 clove garlic, minced
- Salt and black pepper to taste

Instructions:

Prepare Crabmeat:
- Pick through the lump crabmeat to ensure there are no shells or cartilage. Set aside.

Assemble Salad:
- In a large salad bowl, combine the lump crabmeat, diced avocados, halved cherry tomatoes, diced cucumber, and finely chopped red onion.

Make Dressing:
- In a small bowl, whisk together olive oil, fresh lime juice, soy sauce, honey, Dijon mustard, minced garlic, salt, and black pepper.

Dress the Salad:
- Pour the dressing over the crab and avocado mixture. Gently toss the salad to coat everything in the dressing.

Garnish:
- Garnish the salad with fresh cilantro or parsley and sprinkle sesame seeds on top, if desired.

Serve:
- Serve the Avocado and Crab Salad immediately.

This Avocado and Crab Salad is a light and vibrant dish that combines the creaminess of avocados with the sweet and delicate flavor of lump crabmeat. It's perfect for a refreshing lunch, light dinner, or as a side dish for a special occasion. Enjoy!

Grilled Crab Quesadillas

Ingredients:

- 1 pound lump crabmeat, picked over for shells
- 8 large flour tortillas
- 2 cups shredded Monterey Jack cheese
- 1/2 cup diced red bell pepper
- 1/4 cup diced green onions
- 1/4 cup chopped fresh cilantro
- 1 teaspoon ground cumin
- 1 teaspoon chili powder
- 1/2 teaspoon garlic powder
- Juice of 1 lime
- Salt and black pepper to taste
- Olive oil or melted butter for brushing

Instructions:

Prepare Crabmeat:
- Pick through the lump crabmeat to ensure there are no shells or cartilage. Set aside.

Mix Crab Filling:
- In a bowl, combine the lump crabmeat with diced red bell pepper, diced green onions, chopped cilantro, ground cumin, chili powder, garlic powder, lime juice, salt, and black pepper. Mix gently to combine.

Assemble Quesadillas:
- Place a tortilla on a flat surface. Sprinkle a portion of shredded Monterey Jack cheese over half of the tortilla.
- Spoon a generous portion of the crab filling over the cheese.
- Fold the tortilla in half, creating a semi-circle.

Cook on the Grill:
- Preheat your grill or grill pan over medium heat.
- Brush the outer side of each quesadilla with olive oil or melted butter.
- Grill each quesadilla for 2-3 minutes on each side, or until the tortilla is crispy and the cheese is melted.

Serve:
- Remove the quesadillas from the grill and let them rest for a minute.
- Slice the quesadillas into wedges.

Garnish and Enjoy:

- Garnish with additional cilantro, lime wedges, and serve with your favorite dipping sauce (such as salsa or sour cream).

These Grilled Crab Quesadillas are a delightful fusion of flavors with the richness of lump crabmeat, melted cheese, and the added kick of spices. They make for a fantastic appetizer or main course for a seafood-loving crowd. Enjoy!

Cajun Crab Boil

Ingredients:

- 4-5 pounds live blue crabs
- 1 pound large shrimp, peeled and deveined
- 1 pound Andouille sausage, sliced
- 4-6 small red potatoes, halved
- 4 ears of corn, shucked and halved
- 1 onion, quartered
- 1 lemon, halved
- 1 head of garlic, halved horizontally
- 3 bay leaves
- 1/2 cup Cajun seasoning (adjust to taste)
- 1 tablespoon whole black peppercorns
- 1 tablespoon whole coriander seeds
- 1 tablespoon mustard seeds
- Salt to taste
- Hot sauce for serving
- Melted butter for serving

Instructions:

    Prepare Crab and Vegetables:
- Rinse the live crabs thoroughly under cold running water. Remove any visible debris.
- Cut the corn and red potatoes into halves.
- Quarter the onion and halve the lemon.
- Halve the head of garlic horizontally.

    Fill a Large Pot:
- Fill a large stockpot with water, leaving enough room for the ingredients.

    Add Seasonings:
- To the pot, add Cajun seasoning, whole black peppercorns, coriander seeds, mustard seeds, bay leaves, and salt.

    Bring to a Boil:
- Bring the seasoned water to a boil. Allow the flavors to meld for about 10-15 minutes.

    Boil Potatoes and Corn:
- Add the halved potatoes and corn to the boiling water. Cook for about 10-12 minutes or until they are almost tender.

Add Crab, Shrimp, Sausage, and Aromatics:
- Add the live crabs, peeled and deveined shrimp, sliced Andouille sausage, quartered onion, halved lemon, and halved head of garlic to the pot.

Continue Cooking:
- Continue cooking for an additional 10-15 minutes until the crabs turn bright orange, the shrimp are pink and opaque, and the potatoes and corn are fully cooked.

Drain and Serve:
- Using a slotted spoon or drain basket, remove the seafood and vegetables from the pot and transfer them to a large serving platter or table covered with newspapers.

Serve with Condiments:
- Serve the Cajun Crab Boil with hot sauce and melted butter on the side.

Enjoy:
- Dig in and enjoy the Cajun Crab Boil with your hands! Don't forget to have plenty of napkins on hand.

This Cajun Crab Boil is a festive and communal way to enjoy a variety of seafood and vegetables infused with bold Cajun flavors. It's perfect for gatherings and celebrations. Enjoy the feast!

Lobster Recipes:
Lobster Mac and Cheese

Ingredients:

- 8 oz macaroni or pasta of your choice
- 1 1/2 cups cooked lobster meat, chopped into bite-sized pieces
- 1/4 cup unsalted butter
- 1/4 cup all-purpose flour
- 2 cups whole milk
- 1 cup heavy cream
- 2 1/2 cups shredded sharp cheddar cheese
- 1/2 cup shredded Gruyere cheese
- 1/2 cup grated Parmesan cheese
- 1/2 teaspoon dry mustard
- 1/4 teaspoon cayenne pepper
- Salt and black pepper to taste
- 1/2 cup breadcrumbs (for topping)
- Fresh parsley, chopped (for garnish)

Instructions:

Cook the Pasta:
- Cook the macaroni or pasta according to the package instructions. Drain and set aside.

Preheat Oven:
- Preheat your oven to 375°F (190°C).

Prepare Cheese Sauce:
- In a large saucepan, melt the butter over medium heat. Stir in the flour to create a roux. Cook for 1-2 minutes, stirring constantly.
- Gradually whisk in the whole milk and heavy cream. Continue whisking until the mixture thickens.
- Reduce the heat to low, and add the shredded cheddar, Gruyere, and grated Parmesan cheeses. Stir until the cheeses are melted and the sauce is smooth.
- Add the dry mustard, cayenne pepper, salt, and black pepper. Adjust seasonings to taste.

Combine Pasta and Lobster:

- Add the cooked pasta and chopped lobster meat to the cheese sauce. Gently fold until the pasta and lobster are well coated.

Transfer to Baking Dish:
- Transfer the mixture to a greased baking dish.

Prepare Topping:
- In a small bowl, combine the breadcrumbs with a little melted butter. Sprinkle the breadcrumb mixture over the top of the mac and cheese.

Bake:
- Bake in the preheated oven for 25-30 minutes or until the top is golden brown and the cheese is bubbly.

Garnish and Serve:
- Remove from the oven and let it cool for a few minutes. Garnish with chopped fresh parsley.

Serve Warm:
- Serve the Lobster Mac and Cheese warm as a luxurious and indulgent dish.

This Lobster Mac and Cheese is a rich and flavorful treat, combining the creamy goodness of the cheese sauce with succulent lobster. It's a perfect dish for special occasions or when you're craving a comforting and decadent meal. Enjoy!

Lobster Bisque

Ingredients:

- 2 lobster tails, shells removed and meat chopped
- 1/4 cup unsalted butter
- 1 onion, finely chopped
- 2 carrots, peeled and finely chopped
- 2 celery stalks, finely chopped
- 1/4 cup all-purpose flour
- 2 tablespoons tomato paste
- 4 cups fish or seafood stock
- 1 cup dry white wine
- 1 cup heavy cream
- 1 teaspoon paprika
- 1/4 teaspoon cayenne pepper
- Salt and black pepper to taste
- 2 tablespoons brandy (optional)
- Fresh chives or parsley, chopped (for garnish)

Instructions:

Sauté Lobster and Vegetables:
- In a large pot, melt the butter over medium heat. Add the chopped lobster meat, onion, carrots, and celery. Sauté for about 5-7 minutes until the vegetables are softened and the lobster is cooked.

Add Flour and Tomato Paste:
- Sprinkle the flour over the lobster and vegetables. Stir well to combine. Add the tomato paste and continue to cook for another 2-3 minutes.

Deglaze with Wine:
- Pour in the dry white wine to deglaze the pot, scraping up any browned bits from the bottom.

Add Stock:
- Gradually add the fish or seafood stock while stirring to avoid lumps. Bring the mixture to a simmer.

Blend and Strain:
- Use an immersion blender to blend the soup until smooth. Alternatively, transfer the mixture to a blender and blend in batches. Strain the mixture through a fine-mesh sieve to remove any solids.

Add Cream and Seasonings:

- Return the soup to the pot over low heat. Stir in the heavy cream, paprika, cayenne pepper, salt, and black pepper. Allow it to simmer for another 10-15 minutes.

Add Brandy (Optional):
- If using brandy, add it to the bisque and stir well. Allow the flavors to meld for an additional 5 minutes.

Garnish and Serve:
- Ladle the Lobster Bisque into bowls. Garnish with chopped fresh chives or parsley.

Serve Warm:
- Serve the Lobster Bisque warm, and enjoy the rich and luxurious flavors.

This Lobster Bisque is a velvety and indulgent soup that makes for an elegant starter or a comforting meal. It's perfect for special occasions or when you want to treat yourself to a taste of seafood luxury. Enjoy!

Grilled Lobster Tails with Garlic Butter

Ingredients:

- 4 lobster tails
- 1/2 cup unsalted butter, melted
- 4 cloves garlic, minced
- 2 tablespoons fresh parsley, chopped
- 1 tablespoon fresh lemon juice
- Salt and black pepper to taste
- Lemon wedges (for serving)

Instructions:

Preheat Grill:
- Preheat your grill to medium-high heat.

Prepare Lobster Tails:
- Using kitchen shears, carefully cut through the top shell of each lobster tail lengthwise, stopping at the tail fan. Do not cut through the bottom shell.
- Gently spread the lobster tails open without detaching the meat from the bottom shell.

Make Garlic Butter:
- In a small bowl, mix melted butter, minced garlic, chopped fresh parsley, fresh lemon juice, salt, and black pepper.

Brush Lobster Tails:
- Brush the lobster tails with the garlic butter mixture, ensuring that the meat is well coated.

Grill Lobster Tails:
- Place the lobster tails on the preheated grill, shell side down.
- Grill for 8-10 minutes, basting with the garlic butter mixture throughout the cooking process. The lobster meat should be opaque and firm.

Serve:
- Transfer the grilled lobster tails to a serving platter.

Garnish:
- Garnish the lobster tails with additional chopped parsley and serve with lemon wedges on the side.

Enjoy:
- Serve the Grilled Lobster Tails with Garlic Butter immediately, and enjoy this delicious and elegant seafood dish!

Grilling lobster tails with garlic butter imparts a smoky flavor to the sweet lobster meat, creating a mouthwatering dish that's perfect for special occasions or a luxurious meal. Enjoy the rich and succulent taste!

Lobster Roll

Ingredients:

- 4 lobster tails, cooked and chopped
- 1/2 cup mayonnaise
- 1 celery stalk, finely chopped
- 2 tablespoons fresh chives, chopped
- 1 tablespoon fresh lemon juice
- Salt and black pepper to taste
- 4 New England-style split-top hot dog rolls
- Butter for toasting the rolls
- Shredded lettuce (optional)
- Extra chives for garnish

Instructions:

Cook and Chop Lobster Tails:
- Cook the lobster tails according to your preferred method (boiling, steaming, or baking). Once cooked, remove the meat from the shells and chop it into bite-sized pieces.

Make Lobster Salad:
- In a bowl, combine the chopped lobster meat, mayonnaise, finely chopped celery, fresh chives, and fresh lemon juice. Mix well to coat the lobster evenly. Season with salt and black pepper to taste.

Toast the Rolls:
- Heat a skillet or griddle over medium heat. Spread butter on the outsides of the split-top hot dog rolls. Toast them on the skillet until they are golden brown on both sides.

Assemble Lobster Rolls:
- If using, place a layer of shredded lettuce on the toasted rolls.
- Spoon the lobster salad into each roll, filling them generously with the delicious lobster mixture.

Garnish:
- Garnish the lobster rolls with extra chopped chives for a burst of freshness.

Serve:
- Serve the Lobster Rolls immediately, and enjoy the taste of this classic New England treat!

Lobster Rolls are a quintessential summer dish, known for their simplicity and the rich flavor of fresh lobster. Whether enjoyed at a seaside picnic or as a delightful lunch, these rolls are a perfect way to savor the sweetness of lobster. Enjoy!

Lobster and Shrimp Paella

Ingredients:

- 1 cup Arborio rice
- 2 lobster tails, split in half
- 1/2 pound large shrimp, peeled and deveined
- 1/2 cup chorizo sausage, sliced
- 1 onion, finely chopped
- 3 cloves garlic, minced
- 1 red bell pepper, diced
- 1 yellow bell pepper, diced
- 1 cup cherry tomatoes, halved
- 1/2 cup frozen peas
- 1 teaspoon smoked paprika
- 1/2 teaspoon saffron threads (optional)
- 4 cups seafood or chicken broth, heated
- 1/2 cup dry white wine
- 2 tablespoons olive oil
- Salt and black pepper to taste
- Fresh parsley, chopped (for garnish)
- Lemon wedges (for serving)

Instructions:

Prepare Saffron (if using):
- If using saffron threads, steep them in a couple of tablespoons of hot broth or water and set aside.

Cook Lobster Tails and Shrimp:
- Preheat your oven to 375°F (190°C).
- Season the lobster tails and shrimp with salt, pepper, and a drizzle of olive oil. Place them on a baking sheet and roast in the oven for about 10-12 minutes until they are cooked. Set aside.

Sauté Chorizo and Vegetables:
- In a paella pan or large skillet, heat olive oil over medium heat. Add the sliced chorizo and sauté until it releases its oils.
- Add chopped onions and garlic to the pan. Cook until the onions are softened.
- Stir in diced red and yellow bell peppers, and cook for an additional 3-4 minutes until the vegetables are tender.

Add Rice and Smoked Paprika:
- Add Arborio rice to the pan, stirring to coat the rice with the oils. Sprinkle smoked paprika over the rice and continue to sauté for 2-3 minutes.

Pour Wine and Saffron:
- Pour dry white wine into the pan, stirring to deglaze and absorb the flavors.
- If using saffron, add the steeped saffron threads to the pan.

Add Broth and Simmer:
- Pour in the hot seafood or chicken broth, stirring well. Bring the mixture to a simmer and let it cook for 15-20 minutes until the rice is almost cooked, stirring occasionally.

Add Tomatoes and Peas:
- Add halved cherry tomatoes and frozen peas to the pan. Stir gently to incorporate them into the rice mixture.

Arrange Lobster and Shrimp:
- Nestle the roasted lobster tails and shrimp into the rice, pressing them slightly into the mixture.

Finish in the Oven:
- Transfer the paella pan to the preheated oven and bake for an additional 10-12 minutes, or until the rice is fully cooked, and the seafood is heated through.

Garnish and Serve:
- Garnish the Lobster and Shrimp Paella with chopped fresh parsley. Serve hot with lemon wedges on the side.

Enjoy this flavorful and seafood-rich Lobster and Shrimp Paella, a dish that captures the essence of Spanish cuisine!

Lobster and Avocado Salad

Ingredients:

For the Salad:

- 2 lobster tails, cooked and chopped
- 2 ripe avocados, diced
- 1 cup cherry tomatoes, halved
- 1/4 cup red onion, finely chopped
- 1/4 cup cucumber, diced
- 1/4 cup fresh cilantro or parsley, chopped
- Mixed salad greens (optional)

For the Dressing:

- 3 tablespoons extra-virgin olive oil
- 2 tablespoons fresh lemon juice
- 1 tablespoon Dijon mustard
- 1 clove garlic, minced
- Salt and black pepper to taste

Instructions:

Cook and Chop Lobster:
- Cook the lobster tails according to your preferred method (boiling, steaming, or baking). Once cooked, remove the meat from the shells and chop it into bite-sized pieces.

Prepare Salad Ingredients:
- In a large bowl, combine the chopped lobster meat, diced avocados, halved cherry tomatoes, finely chopped red onion, diced cucumber, and chopped fresh cilantro or parsley. If desired, add mixed salad greens to the bowl.

Make the Dressing:
- In a small bowl, whisk together extra-virgin olive oil, fresh lemon juice, Dijon mustard, minced garlic, salt, and black pepper. Adjust the seasoning to taste.

Toss Salad with Dressing:
- Drizzle the dressing over the lobster and avocado mixture. Gently toss the salad to coat all ingredients evenly with the dressing.

Serve:

- Arrange the Lobster and Avocado Salad on individual plates or a serving platter.

Garnish and Enjoy:
- Garnish with additional chopped cilantro or parsley if desired. Serve the salad immediately and enjoy the delicious combination of lobster and avocado flavors!

This Lobster and Avocado Salad is a light and refreshing dish that showcases the sweetness of lobster and the creamy texture of avocado. It's perfect for a light lunch, a refreshing appetizer, or a delightful side dish for a special occasion. Enjoy!

Lobster and Asparagus Risotto

Ingredients:

For the Salad:

- 2 lobster tails, cooked and chopped
- 2 ripe avocados, diced
- 1 cup cherry tomatoes, halved
- 1/4 cup red onion, finely chopped
- 1/4 cup cucumber, diced
- 1/4 cup fresh cilantro or parsley, chopped
- Mixed salad greens (optional)

For the Dressing:

- 3 tablespoons extra-virgin olive oil
- 2 tablespoons fresh lemon juice
- 1 tablespoon Dijon mustard
- 1 clove garlic, minced
- Salt and black pepper to taste

Instructions:

Cook and Chop Lobster:
- Cook the lobster tails according to your preferred method (boiling, steaming, or baking). Once cooked, remove the meat from the shells and chop it into bite-sized pieces.

Prepare Salad Ingredients:
- In a large bowl, combine the chopped lobster meat, diced avocados, halved cherry tomatoes, finely chopped red onion, diced cucumber, and chopped fresh cilantro or parsley. If desired, add mixed salad greens to the bowl.

Make the Dressing:
- In a small bowl, whisk together extra-virgin olive oil, fresh lemon juice, Dijon mustard, minced garlic, salt, and black pepper. Adjust the seasoning to taste.

Toss Salad with Dressing:
- Drizzle the dressing over the lobster and avocado mixture. Gently toss the salad to coat all ingredients evenly with the dressing.

Serve:
- Arrange the Lobster and Avocado Salad on individual plates or a serving platter.

Garnish and Enjoy:
- Garnish with additional chopped cilantro or parsley if desired. Serve the salad immediately and enjoy the delicious combination of lobster and avocado flavors!

This Lobster and Avocado Salad is a light and refreshing dish that showcases the sweetness of lobster and the creamy texture of avocado. It's perfect for a light lunch, a refreshing appetizer, or a delightful side dish for a special occasion. Enjoy!

Lobster and Asparagus Risotto

Ingredients:

- 2 lobster tails, cooked and chopped
- 1 cup Arborio rice
- 1/2 cup dry white wine
- 4 cups chicken or seafood broth, warmed
- 1 cup asparagus, trimmed and cut into bite-sized pieces
- 1/2 cup Parmesan cheese, grated
- 1/4 cup shallots, finely chopped
- 2 cloves garlic, minced
- 2 tablespoons olive oil
- 2 tablespoons unsalted butter
- Salt and black pepper to taste
- Fresh parsley, chopped (for garnish)
- Lemon wedges (for serving)

Instructions:

Cook Lobster Tails:
- Cook the lobster tails according to your preferred method (boiling, steaming, or baking). Once cooked, remove the meat from the shells and chop it into bite-sized pieces.

Sauté Shallots and Garlic:
- In a large skillet or risotto pan, heat olive oil and 1 tablespoon of butter over medium heat. Add finely chopped shallots and minced garlic. Sauté until the shallots are translucent.

Toast Arborio Rice:
- Add Arborio rice to the pan, stirring to coat the rice with the oil and butter. Toast the rice for 2-3 minutes until it becomes slightly translucent.

Deglaze with Wine:
- Pour in the dry white wine and stir until the wine is mostly absorbed by the rice.

Add Broth:
- Begin adding the warmed chicken or seafood broth, one ladle at a time. Allow the liquid to be mostly absorbed before adding the next ladle. Stir frequently.

Cook Asparagus:
- When the rice is halfway cooked, add the chopped asparagus to the risotto. Continue adding broth and stirring until the rice and asparagus are tender.

Finish Risotto:
- Once the risotto is cooked to your desired consistency, stir in the chopped lobster meat.

- Add grated Parmesan cheese and the remaining tablespoon of butter. Season with salt and black pepper to taste. Stir until the cheese and butter are melted and well combined.

Garnish and Serve:
- Garnish the Lobster and Asparagus Risotto with chopped fresh parsley. Serve hot with lemon wedges on the side.

Enjoy:
- Enjoy this luxurious Lobster and Asparagus Risotto as a flavorful and comforting dish!

This Lobster and Asparagus Risotto is a delightful combination of creamy rice, sweet lobster, and vibrant asparagus. It makes for an impressive and delicious meal, perfect for special occasions or a gourmet dinner at home. Enjoy!

Lobster Newberg

Ingredients:

- 2 lobster tails, cooked and meat removed, chopped into bite-sized pieces
- 4 tablespoons unsalted butter
- 2 tablespoons all-purpose flour
- 1 cup heavy cream
- 3 egg yolks
- 1/4 cup dry sherry
- Salt and cayenne pepper to taste
- 1 tablespoon brandy (optional)
- Chopped fresh chives or parsley (for garnish)
- Toast points or buttered toast (for serving)

Instructions:

Cook Lobster Tails:
- Cook the lobster tails according to your preferred method (boiling, steaming, or baking). Once cooked, remove the meat from the shells and chop it into bite-sized pieces.

Make the Sauce:
- In a saucepan, melt 2 tablespoons of butter over medium heat. Stir in the flour to create a roux, cooking for 1-2 minutes.
- Slowly add the heavy cream, stirring constantly to avoid lumps. Cook until the mixture thickens.

Temper the Egg Yolks:
- In a separate bowl, beat the egg yolks. Gradually add a small amount of the hot cream mixture to the egg yolks, stirring constantly. This process, known as tempering, prevents the eggs from scrambling when added to the hot sauce.

Combine Egg Yolks with Sauce:
- Slowly pour the tempered egg yolks back into the saucepan, stirring continuously. Cook for an additional 2-3 minutes until the sauce thickens further.

Add Sherry and Seasonings:
- Stir in the dry sherry and chopped lobster meat. Season with salt and a pinch of cayenne pepper to taste.

Finish with Brandy (Optional):

- If using brandy, add it to the sauce and stir well. Allow the sauce to simmer for another 2-3 minutes.

Serve:
- Remove the saucepan from heat and stir in the remaining 2 tablespoons of butter.
- Spoon the Lobster Newberg over toast points or buttered toast.

Garnish and Enjoy:
- Garnish with chopped fresh chives or parsley. Serve immediately and enjoy the rich and indulgent flavors.

Lobster Newberg is a classic dish known for its creamy, flavorful sauce. It's a perfect choice for a special occasion or an elegant dinner at home. Enjoy this timeless recipe!

Lobster and Mango Salsa Tacos

Ingredients:

For the Lobster Filling:

- 2 lobster tails, cooked and meat removed, chopped into bite-sized pieces
- 2 tablespoons unsalted butter
- 1 clove garlic, minced
- 1 teaspoon chili powder
- Salt and black pepper to taste
- Juice of 1 lime

For the Mango Salsa:

- 1 ripe mango, peeled, pitted, and diced
- 1/2 red onion, finely chopped
- 1 jalapeño, seeds removed and finely chopped
- 1/4 cup fresh cilantro, chopped
- Juice of 1 lime
- Salt to taste

For Serving:

- Small flour or corn tortillas
- Shredded lettuce or cabbage
- Avocado slices (optional)
- Lime wedges
- Fresh cilantro for garnish

Instructions:

Prepare Lobster Filling:
- In a skillet, melt butter over medium heat. Add minced garlic and sauté until fragrant.
- Add chopped lobster meat to the skillet. Sprinkle with chili powder, salt, and black pepper. Cook for 2-3 minutes until the lobster is heated through.
- Squeeze lime juice over the lobster and toss to combine. Remove from heat and set aside.

Make Mango Salsa:

- In a bowl, combine diced mango, finely chopped red onion, jalapeño, chopped cilantro, lime juice, and a pinch of salt. Mix well to create the mango salsa.

Warm Tortillas:
- Heat the tortillas in a dry skillet or warm them in the oven according to the package instructions.

Assemble Tacos:
- Place a spoonful of the lobster filling on each tortilla.
- Top with shredded lettuce or cabbage, a spoonful of mango salsa, and avocado slices if using.

Garnish and Serve:
- Garnish the Lobster and Mango Salsa Tacos with fresh cilantro. Serve with lime wedges on the side.

Enjoy:
- Enjoy these delicious and flavorful tacos with the perfect balance of sweet and savory flavors!

These Lobster and Mango Salsa Tacos are a delightful fusion of seafood, vibrant fruits, and zesty flavors. They make for a fresh and satisfying meal, perfect for a summer gathering or any occasion. Enjoy the tropical goodness!

Lobster Thermidor

Ingredients:

For the Lobster Filling:

- 2 lobster tails, cooked and meat removed, chopped into bite-sized pieces
- 2 tablespoons unsalted butter
- 1/4 cup shallots, finely chopped
- 2 cloves garlic, minced
- 2 tablespoons all-purpose flour
- 1/2 cup dry white wine
- 1 cup heavy cream
- 2 tablespoons Dijon mustard
- 2 tablespoons fresh tarragon, chopped
- Salt and black pepper to taste
- 1 tablespoon brandy (optional)
- Grated Parmesan cheese for topping

For the Topping:

- 1/2 cup breadcrumbs
- 2 tablespoons unsalted butter, melted

For Serving:

- Cooked rice or toasted baguette slices
- Fresh parsley, chopped (for garnish)

Instructions:

Prepare Lobster Filling:

- In a large skillet, melt 2 tablespoons of butter over medium heat. Add chopped shallots and minced garlic. Sauté until softened.
- Sprinkle flour over the shallot mixture and stir well to create a roux. Cook for 1-2 minutes.
- Pour in the dry white wine and whisk to combine. Allow the mixture to thicken.
- Gradually add the heavy cream, Dijon mustard, chopped tarragon, salt, and black pepper. Stir until the sauce is smooth.
- If using brandy, add it to the sauce and stir well.
- Add the chopped lobster meat to the sauce, coating it evenly. Cook for an additional 2-3 minutes until the lobster is heated through.

Prepare Topping:

- In a small bowl, mix breadcrumbs with melted butter.

Assemble and Bake:

- Preheat your oven's broiler.
- Transfer the lobster mixture to individual ovenproof dishes or a baking dish.
- Sprinkle the breadcrumb topping over the lobster filling.
- Place the dishes under the broiler for 2-3 minutes or until the breadcrumbs are golden brown and the sauce is bubbly.

Serve:

- Remove from the oven and let it cool for a couple of minutes.
- Serve the Lobster Thermidor over cooked rice or toasted baguette slices.

Garnish and Enjoy:

- Garnish with chopped fresh parsley. Enjoy the decadent Lobster Thermidor!

Lobster Thermidor is a luxurious dish that combines the sweetness of lobster with a rich and flavorful creamy sauce. It's perfect for special occasions or a gourmet dinner at home. Enjoy this classic French delicacy!

Mixed Seafood Recipes:
Seafood Paella

Ingredients:

- 1 cup Arborio rice
- 8 large shrimp, peeled and deveined
- 8 small clams or mussels, scrubbed and debearded
- 1/2 pound squid, cleaned and sliced into rings
- 1/2 pound firm white fish (such as cod or haddock), cut into bite-sized pieces
- 1/2 cup cooked crab meat (optional)
- 1 onion, finely chopped
- 4 cloves garlic, minced
- 1 red bell pepper, diced
- 1 tomato, diced
- 1/2 cup frozen peas
- 4 cups seafood or chicken broth, warmed
- 1/2 cup dry white wine
- 1 teaspoon saffron threads
- 1 teaspoon smoked paprika
- Salt and black pepper to taste
- 1/4 cup fresh parsley, chopped
- Lemon wedges (for serving)
- Olive oil for cooking

Instructions:

Infuse Saffron:
- In a small bowl, combine saffron threads with warm seafood or chicken broth. Let it sit and infuse while you prepare the other ingredients.

Prepare Seafood:
- Season the shrimp, squid, clams or mussels, and white fish with salt and pepper.

Sauté Seafood:
- In a large paella pan or wide skillet, heat olive oil over medium-high heat. Sear the shrimp until pink on both sides. Remove and set aside.
- Sauté the squid rings until just cooked. Remove and set aside.
- Add a bit more oil if needed and sear the white fish until golden. Remove and set aside.

- Add a bit more oil and briefly sauté the clams or mussels until they start to open. Remove and set aside.

Sauté Aromatics:
- In the same pan, add chopped onions, diced red bell pepper, and minced garlic. Sauté until the vegetables are softened.

Add Rice and Paprika:
- Stir in the Arborio rice and smoked paprika. Cook for 2-3 minutes until the rice is well-coated and slightly translucent.

Deglaze with Wine:
- Pour in the dry white wine and cook for a couple of minutes until the wine is mostly absorbed.

Add Tomatoes and Peas:
- Add diced tomatoes and frozen peas to the pan. Stir to combine.

Pour in Infused Broth:
- Pour in the saffron-infused broth, including the saffron threads. Stir well to distribute the ingredients evenly.

Simmer and Arrange Seafood:
- Bring the mixture to a simmer and let it cook for about 15-20 minutes or until the rice is almost cooked, stirring occasionally.
- Arrange the seared seafood (shrimp, squid, white fish, clams or mussels) over the rice.

Finish Cooking:
- Continue cooking for an additional 10-15 minutes until the rice is fully cooked and has formed a crust at the bottom (known as "socarrat").

Garnish and Serve:
- Sprinkle chopped fresh parsley over the paella. Serve with lemon wedges on the side.

Enjoy:
- Serve the Seafood Paella directly from the pan, allowing everyone to dig in and enjoy the flavors.

Seafood Paella is a festive and communal dish that captures the essence of Spanish cuisine. It's perfect for gatherings and celebrations. Enjoy this delicious and visually stunning seafood feast!

Cioppino (Italian Seafood Stew)

Ingredients:

For the Base:

- 2 tablespoons olive oil
- 1 large onion, finely chopped
- 4 cloves garlic, minced
- 1 red bell pepper, diced
- 1 fennel bulb, thinly sliced
- 1 teaspoon dried oregano
- 1 teaspoon dried basil
- 1/2 teaspoon red pepper flakes (adjust to taste)
- Salt and black pepper to taste
- 1 cup dry white wine
- 1 can (28 ounces) crushed tomatoes
- 1 can (14 ounces) diced tomatoes
- 4 cups fish or seafood broth
- 1 bay leaf

For the Seafood:

- 1 pound firm white fish (such as halibut or cod), cut into chunks
- 1/2 pound large shrimp, peeled and deveined
- 1/2 pound mussels, cleaned and debearded
- 1/2 pound clams, scrubbed
- 1/2 pound crab legs or crab meat
- 1/2 pound calamari (squid), cleaned and sliced into rings

For Garnish:

- Fresh parsley, chopped
- Toasted bread or baguette slices

Instructions:

Sauté Aromatics:
- In a large pot or Dutch oven, heat olive oil over medium heat. Add chopped onion, minced garlic, diced red bell pepper, and sliced fennel. Sauté until the vegetables are softened.

Season and Deglaze:
- Add dried oregano, dried basil, red pepper flakes, salt, and black pepper. Stir well to coat the vegetables.
- Pour in the dry white wine to deglaze the pot, scraping up any browned bits from the bottom.

Add Tomatoes and Broth:
- Add crushed tomatoes, diced tomatoes, fish or seafood broth, and the bay leaf to the pot. Stir to combine.

Simmer the Base:
- Bring the mixture to a simmer, then reduce the heat to low. Let it simmer for about 20-30 minutes to allow the flavors to meld.

Prepare Seafood:
- Season the fish chunks, shrimp, mussels, clams, crab legs or meat, and calamari with salt and pepper.

Add Seafood to the Stew:
- Add the seasoned seafood to the simmering broth. Arrange the seafood evenly in the pot.
- Cover and let the seafood cook for about 10-15 minutes, or until the mussels and clams open, the fish flakes easily, and the shrimp turns pink.

Discard Bay Leaf and Serve:
- Discard the bay leaf from the stew.
- Ladle the Cioppino into bowls, making sure to distribute a variety of seafood in each serving.

Garnish and Enjoy:
- Garnish with chopped fresh parsley.
- Serve the Cioppino hot with toasted bread or baguette slices on the side.

Cioppino is a comforting and flavorful seafood stew that is perfect for a festive meal or a special occasion. Enjoy the rich and robust flavors of this Italian-American classic!

Seafood Gumbo

Ingredients:

For the Roux:

- 1 cup all-purpose flour
- 1 cup vegetable oil

For the Gumbo:

- 1 large onion, finely chopped
- 1 bell pepper, diced
- 2 celery stalks, diced
- 4 cloves garlic, minced
- 1 pound andouille sausage, sliced
- 1 pound okra, sliced (fresh or frozen)
- 1 can (14 ounces) diced tomatoes
- 8 cups seafood or chicken broth
- 1 bay leaf
- 1 teaspoon dried thyme
- 1 teaspoon dried oregano
- 1 teaspoon smoked paprika
- 1/2 teaspoon cayenne pepper (adjust to taste)
- Salt and black pepper to taste
- 1 pound shrimp, peeled and deveined
- 1 pound crab meat
- 1 pound fresh or frozen crawfish tails
- 1/2 cup fresh parsley, chopped
- 1/4 cup green onions, sliced
- Cooked white rice (for serving)

Instructions:

Prepare the Roux:
- In a large, heavy-bottomed pot or Dutch oven, combine flour and vegetable oil to make the roux. Cook over medium heat, stirring constantly, until the roux reaches a dark, chocolate brown color. Be attentive to avoid burning. This may take about 30-45 minutes.

Sauté Vegetables and Sausage:

- Add chopped onion, diced bell pepper, diced celery, and minced garlic to the roux. Cook for 5-7 minutes, stirring frequently.
- Add sliced andouille sausage and continue to cook for an additional 5 minutes until the sausage is browned.

Add Okra and Tomatoes:
- Stir in sliced okra and diced tomatoes. Cook for another 5 minutes, allowing the okra to soften.

Pour in Broth:
- Slowly pour in seafood or chicken broth while stirring continuously to avoid lumps. Add bay leaf, dried thyme, dried oregano, smoked paprika, cayenne pepper, salt, and black pepper.

Simmer Gumbo:
- Bring the gumbo to a simmer. Let it cook uncovered for about 30-45 minutes, allowing the flavors to meld and the gumbo to thicken.

Add Seafood:
- Add peeled and deveined shrimp, crab meat, and crawfish tails to the pot. Cook for an additional 10-15 minutes, or until the seafood is cooked through.

Adjust Seasoning:
- Taste the gumbo and adjust the seasoning as needed. Add more salt, pepper, or cayenne pepper according to your preference.

Finish and Serve:
- Stir in chopped fresh parsley and sliced green onions.
- Serve the Seafood Gumbo over cooked white rice.

Garnish and Enjoy:
- Garnish with additional parsley and green onions if desired.

Seafood Gumbo is a delightful and comforting dish that showcases the diverse flavors of the Gulf Coast. Enjoy this flavorful stew with a side of rice for a truly satisfying meal!

Thai Seafood Curry

Ingredients:

For the Curry Paste:

- 2 tablespoons red curry paste
- 1 tablespoon lemongrass, minced
- 1 tablespoon ginger, minced
- 4 cloves garlic, minced
- 2 tablespoons cilantro stems, finely chopped
- 1 teaspoon shrimp paste (optional, for added depth of flavor)

For the Curry:

- 1 pound mixed seafood (shrimp, squid, mussels, fish fillets, etc.)
- 1 can (14 ounces) coconut milk
- 1 cup seafood or vegetable broth
- 1 red bell pepper, sliced
- 1 zucchini, sliced
- 1 carrot, julienned
- 1 onion, sliced
- 1 tablespoon vegetable oil
- 2 tablespoons fish sauce
- 1 tablespoon soy sauce
- 1 tablespoon brown sugar
- Juice of 1 lime
- Fresh cilantro leaves for garnish
- Thai basil leaves for garnish
- Cooked jasmine rice (for serving)

Instructions:

Prepare Curry Paste:
- In a mortar and pestle or a food processor, combine all the curry paste ingredients (red curry paste, lemongrass, ginger, garlic, cilantro stems, and shrimp paste). Grind or process until you have a smooth paste.

Sauté Curry Paste:
- Heat vegetable oil in a large pan or wok over medium heat. Add the curry paste and sauté for 1-2 minutes until it becomes fragrant.

Add Vegetables:

- Add sliced red bell pepper, zucchini, carrot, and onion to the pan. Stir-fry for 3-5 minutes until the vegetables begin to soften.

Pour in Coconut Milk and Broth:
- Pour in the coconut milk and seafood or vegetable broth. Stir well to combine.

Season the Curry:
- Add fish sauce, soy sauce, and brown sugar to the pan. Stir to incorporate the flavors.

Add Seafood:
- Add the mixed seafood to the pan. Cook for 5-7 minutes until the seafood is cooked through.

Finish and Adjust:
- Squeeze the juice of one lime into the curry. Taste and adjust the seasoning, adding more fish sauce, soy sauce, or sugar as needed.

Serve:
- Serve the Thai Seafood Curry over cooked jasmine rice.

Garnish and Enjoy:
- Garnish with fresh cilantro leaves and Thai basil leaves.

Thai Seafood Curry is a delightful and aromatic dish with a perfect balance of spiciness, sweetness, and creaminess. It's a comforting and satisfying meal that brings the flavors of Thai cuisine to your table. Enjoy!

Mediterranean Seafood Pasta

Ingredients:

- 8 ounces linguine or spaghetti
- 2 tablespoons olive oil
- 4 cloves garlic, minced
- 1 small onion, finely chopped
- 1 red bell pepper, sliced
- 1 yellow bell pepper, sliced
- 1 cup cherry tomatoes, halved
- 1/2 cup Kalamata olives, pitted and sliced
- 1/2 cup artichoke hearts, quartered
- 1 pound mixed seafood (shrimp, mussels, calamari, etc.)
- 1/2 cup dry white wine
- 1 can (14 ounces) diced tomatoes, undrained
- 1 teaspoon dried oregano
- 1 teaspoon dried basil
- Salt and black pepper to taste
- Crushed red pepper flakes (optional, for added heat)
- Fresh parsley, chopped (for garnish)
- Grated Parmesan cheese (for serving)

Instructions:

Cook Pasta:
- Cook the pasta according to package instructions until al dente. Drain and set aside.

Sauté Aromatics:
- In a large skillet, heat olive oil over medium heat. Add minced garlic and chopped onion. Sauté until the onion becomes translucent.

Add Vegetables:
- Add sliced red and yellow bell peppers, halved cherry tomatoes, Kalamata olives, and quartered artichoke hearts to the skillet. Cook for 5-7 minutes until the vegetables are tender.

Cook Seafood:
- Add the mixed seafood to the skillet. Cook for 3-5 minutes or until the seafood is just cooked through.

Deglaze with Wine:

- Pour in the dry white wine to deglaze the pan, scraping up any browned bits from the bottom.

Add Tomatoes and Seasoning:
- Stir in the diced tomatoes with their juice. Season the mixture with dried oregano, dried basil, salt, black pepper, and red pepper flakes if using.

Simmer:
- Let the sauce simmer for 10-15 minutes to allow the flavors to meld.

Combine with Pasta:
- Add the cooked pasta to the skillet, tossing it with the seafood and vegetable mixture until well combined.

Garnish and Serve:
- Garnish with chopped fresh parsley.
- Serve the Mediterranean Seafood Pasta hot, and sprinkle with grated Parmesan cheese if desired.

Enjoy:
- Enjoy the delightful flavors of the Mediterranean in this savory and satisfying seafood pasta dish!

Mediterranean Seafood Pasta is a perfect blend of seafood, vibrant vegetables, and aromatic herbs. It's a wonderful dish that captures the essence of Mediterranean cuisine. Buon appetito!

Seafood Enchiladas

Ingredients:

For the Enchilada Filling:

- 1 pound mixed seafood (shrimp, crab, and/or scallops), peeled, deveined, and chopped
- 1 tablespoon olive oil
- 1 small onion, finely chopped
- 2 cloves garlic, minced
- 1 bell pepper, diced
- 1 teaspoon ground cumin
- 1 teaspoon chili powder
- Salt and black pepper to taste
- Juice of 1 lime
- 1/2 cup fresh cilantro, chopped

For the Enchilada Sauce:

- 2 tablespoons olive oil
- 2 tablespoons all-purpose flour
- 2 tablespoons chili powder
- 1 teaspoon ground cumin
- 1 teaspoon dried oregano
- 1/2 teaspoon garlic powder
- 2 cups chicken or vegetable broth
- Salt to taste

Other Ingredients:

- 8 small flour tortillas
- 2 cups shredded Monterey Jack or Mexican blend cheese
- 1/2 cup sour cream (optional, for serving)
- Sliced green onions and fresh cilantro for garnish

Instructions:

Prepare the Enchilada Filling:
- In a skillet, heat olive oil over medium heat. Add chopped onion, minced garlic, and diced bell pepper. Sauté until the vegetables are softened.

- Add the mixed seafood to the skillet and cook until just opaque.
- Season with ground cumin, chili powder, salt, and black pepper. Stir in the lime juice and fresh cilantro. Cook for an additional 2-3 minutes. Remove from heat and set aside.

Make the Enchilada Sauce:
- In a saucepan, heat olive oil over medium heat. Stir in all-purpose flour, chili powder, ground cumin, dried oregano, and garlic powder. Cook for 1-2 minutes to create a roux.
- Slowly whisk in chicken or vegetable broth, ensuring there are no lumps. Continue whisking until the sauce thickens. Add salt to taste. Simmer for 5-7 minutes. Set aside.

Assemble the Enchiladas:
- Preheat the oven to 375°F (190°C).
- Spread a small amount of enchilada sauce on the bottom of a baking dish.
- Spoon the seafood filling onto each flour tortilla and roll it up. Place the enchiladas seam side down in the baking dish.
- Pour the remaining enchilada sauce over the top of the enchiladas, covering them evenly.

Bake:
- Sprinkle shredded cheese over the enchiladas.
- Bake in the preheated oven for 20-25 minutes or until the cheese is melted and bubbly.

Serve:
- Remove from the oven and let it cool slightly before serving.
- Garnish with sliced green onions, fresh cilantro, and a dollop of sour cream if desired.

Enjoy:
- Serve the seafood enchiladas warm and enjoy the delicious combination of flavors.

These seafood enchiladas are a delightful fusion of Mexican and seafood flavors. They make for a satisfying and flavorful meal that's perfect for any occasion. Enjoy!

Seafood Stir-Fry with Vegetables

Ingredients:

For the Stir-Fry:

- 1 pound mixed seafood (shrimp, scallops, squid), cleaned and deveined
- 2 tablespoons soy sauce
- 1 tablespoon oyster sauce
- 1 tablespoon fish sauce
- 1 tablespoon sesame oil
- 2 tablespoons vegetable oil (for cooking)
- 3 cloves garlic, minced
- 1 tablespoon ginger, grated
- 1 bell pepper, sliced
- 1 carrot, julienned
- 1 cup broccoli florets
- 1 cup snap peas, ends trimmed
- 1 cup sliced mushrooms
- 1 cup baby corn, halved
- 1 cup bok choy, chopped
- 1 tablespoon cornstarch (optional, for thickening)

For Serving:

- Cooked rice or noodles

Instructions:

Prepare the Seafood:
- In a bowl, combine the mixed seafood with soy sauce, oyster sauce, and fish sauce. Let it marinate for about 15 minutes.

Heat the Wok or Skillet:
- Heat vegetable oil in a wok or large skillet over medium-high heat.

Cook the Seafood:
- Add minced garlic and grated ginger to the hot oil. Stir-fry for about 30 seconds until fragrant.
- Add the marinated seafood to the wok and stir-fry for 2-3 minutes until the seafood is cooked through. Remove the seafood from the wok and set aside.

Stir-Fry Vegetables:

- In the same wok, add a bit more oil if needed. Stir in bell pepper, carrot, broccoli, snap peas, mushrooms, baby corn, and bok choy. Stir-fry for 4-5 minutes until the vegetables are crisp-tender.

Combine Seafood and Vegetables:
- Return the cooked seafood to the wok with the vegetables. Toss everything together.

Add Sesame Oil:
- Drizzle sesame oil over the stir-fry and toss to coat evenly. This adds a rich, aromatic flavor to the dish.

Optional Cornstarch Slurry:
- If you prefer a thicker sauce, mix cornstarch with a bit of water to create a slurry. Add it to the stir-fry and stir until the sauce thickens.

Serve:
- Serve the seafood and vegetable stir-fry over cooked rice or noodles.

Enjoy:
- Enjoy your delicious and healthy seafood stir-fry!

Feel free to customize the vegetables and seafood based on your preferences. This versatile stir-fry is not only tasty but also a great way to incorporate a variety of colorful and nutritious vegetables into your meal.

Seafood Tostadas

Ingredients:

For the Seafood:

- 1 pound mixed seafood (shrimp, scallops, or any seafood of your choice), cleaned and deveined
- 2 tablespoons olive oil
- 2 cloves garlic, minced
- 1 teaspoon chili powder
- 1 teaspoon ground cumin
- 1/2 teaspoon smoked paprika
- Salt and black pepper to taste
- Juice of 1 lime

For the Tostadas:

- Corn or flour tortillas
- Vegetable oil for frying

Toppings:

- Shredded lettuce or cabbage
- Diced tomatoes
- Sliced avocado
- Sliced radishes
- Chopped cilantro
- Lime wedges

Optional Sauce:

- 1/2 cup sour cream or Greek yogurt
- 1 tablespoon mayonnaise
- Juice of 1 lime
- 1 teaspoon hot sauce (adjust to taste)
- Salt and pepper to taste

Instructions:

Prepare the Seafood:

- In a bowl, combine the cleaned and deveined seafood with olive oil, minced garlic, chili powder, ground cumin, smoked paprika, salt, and black pepper. Toss well to coat the seafood evenly.
- Heat a skillet over medium-high heat. Add the seasoned seafood to the skillet and cook for 3-5 minutes until the seafood is cooked through. Squeeze lime juice over the cooked seafood. Set aside.

Prepare the Tostadas:
- In a separate skillet, heat vegetable oil over medium-high heat. Fry the tortillas until they are golden and crispy. Drain on paper towels.

Optional Sauce:
- In a small bowl, mix sour cream or Greek yogurt, mayonnaise, lime juice, hot sauce, salt, and pepper. This sauce adds a creamy and tangy element to the tostadas.

Assemble the Tostadas:
- Spread a layer of the cooked seafood onto each crispy tortilla.
- Top with shredded lettuce or cabbage, diced tomatoes, sliced avocado, sliced radishes, and chopped cilantro.
- Drizzle the optional sauce over the toppings.

Serve:
- Serve the seafood tostadas immediately, garnished with lime wedges on the side.

Enjoy:
- Enjoy the burst of flavors and textures in each bite of these delicious seafood tostadas!

Seafood tostadas are customizable, so feel free to add your favorite toppings and adjust the spice level to suit your taste. They make for a perfect light and refreshing meal, especially in warmer weather. Buen provecho!

Seafood Kabobs with Lemon Garlic Marinade

Ingredients:

For the Lemon Garlic Marinade:

- 1/4 cup olive oil
- 3 tablespoons fresh lemon juice
- Zest of 1 lemon
- 4 cloves garlic, minced
- 1 teaspoon dried oregano
- 1 teaspoon dried thyme
- 1 teaspoon paprika
- Salt and black pepper to taste

For the Seafood Kabobs:

- 1 pound mixed seafood (shrimp, scallops, chunks of firm fish like salmon or cod)
- Cherry tomatoes
- Red bell pepper, cut into chunks
- Red onion, cut into chunks
- Wooden or metal skewers

Instructions:

Prepare the Marinade:
- In a bowl, whisk together olive oil, fresh lemon juice, lemon zest, minced garlic, dried oregano, dried thyme, paprika, salt, and black pepper. This creates a flavorful lemon garlic marinade.

Prepare the Seafood:
- If using wooden skewers, soak them in water for at least 30 minutes to prevent burning during grilling.
- Clean and prepare the seafood by peeling and deveining shrimp, and cutting other seafood into bite-sized pieces.

Marinate the Seafood:
- Place the seafood in a bowl and pour the lemon garlic marinade over it. Toss to coat the seafood evenly. Let it marinate for at least 30 minutes, or you can refrigerate it for a few hours for more flavor.

Assemble the Kabobs:
- Preheat the grill to medium-high heat.

- Thread the marinated seafood, cherry tomatoes, red bell pepper chunks, and red onion chunks onto the skewers, alternating them for a colorful presentation.

Grill the Kabobs:
- Place the seafood kabobs on the preheated grill. Cook for 2-3 minutes per side, or until the seafood is cooked through and has grill marks.

Serve:
- Remove the seafood kabobs from the grill and let them rest for a minute.
- Serve the kabobs on a platter, and drizzle any remaining lemon garlic marinade over them.

Garnish and Enjoy:
- Garnish with fresh herbs like parsley or cilantro, and serve the seafood kabobs with additional lemon wedges on the side.

Serving Suggestions:
- Enjoy the kabobs with a side of rice, couscous, or a fresh salad.

These seafood kabobs are not only delicious but also visually appealing. The lemon garlic marinade adds a zesty and aromatic touch, making this a perfect dish for a summer barbecue or any outdoor gathering. Enjoy your flavorful seafood kabobs!

Seafood and Saffron Risotto

Ingredients:

- 1 cup Arborio rice
- 1/2 cup dry white wine
- 4 cups seafood or vegetable broth, kept warm
- 1 small onion, finely chopped
- 2 cloves garlic, minced
- 1/4 cup olive oil
- 1/2 cup dry white wine
- 1/4 teaspoon saffron threads
- 1 pound mixed seafood (shrimp, scallops, mussels, squid), cleaned and prepared
- 1/2 cup Parmesan cheese, grated
- Salt and black pepper to taste
- Fresh parsley, chopped (for garnish)
- Lemon wedges (for serving)

Instructions:

Prepare the Saffron Infusion:
- In a small bowl, combine the saffron threads with 2 tablespoons of warm water. Allow it to steep and infuse its flavor.

Cook the Seafood:
- In a large pan, heat 2 tablespoons of olive oil over medium-high heat. Add the mixed seafood and cook until just opaque and cooked through. Remove from the pan and set aside.

Sauté Onion and Garlic:
- In the same pan, add the remaining 2 tablespoons of olive oil. Sauté the chopped onion and minced garlic until softened.

Toast the Rice:
- Add Arborio rice to the pan and cook, stirring constantly, until the rice is well-coated with the oil and slightly toasted.

Deglaze with White Wine:
- Pour in the dry white wine, stirring continuously until it is mostly absorbed by the rice.

Add Saffron Infusion:
- Add the saffron infusion to the rice and continue stirring. The saffron will impart its vibrant color and aroma to the dish.

Start Adding Broth:

- Begin adding the warm seafood or vegetable broth, one ladle at a time. Allow each ladleful to be absorbed by the rice before adding the next.

Continue Cooking:
- Continue this process of adding broth and stirring until the rice is creamy and cooked to al dente. This should take about 18-20 minutes.

Finish the Risotto:
- Once the rice is cooked, stir in the cooked seafood and grated Parmesan cheese. Season with salt and black pepper to taste.

Garnish and Serve:
- Garnish the seafood and saffron risotto with chopped fresh parsley.
- Serve the risotto hot, with lemon wedges on the side for an extra burst of citrus flavor.

Enjoy:
- Enjoy the rich and savory flavors of this seafood and saffron risotto!

This dish is perfect for a special occasion or a romantic dinner. The saffron adds a unique and elegant touch, complementing the seafood and creating a dish that's both visually stunning and delicious. Buon appetito!

Fish Tacos:
Grilled Fish Tacos with Cilantro Lime Slaw

Ingredients:

For the Grilled Fish:

- 1.5 pounds white fish fillets (tilapia, cod, or mahi-mahi)
- 2 tablespoons olive oil
- 1 teaspoon ground cumin
- 1 teaspoon chili powder
- 1/2 teaspoon garlic powder
- 1/2 teaspoon onion powder
- Salt and black pepper to taste
- Juice of 1 lime

For the Cilantro Lime Slaw:

- 2 cups shredded green cabbage
- 1 cup shredded purple cabbage
- 1/2 cup thinly sliced red onion
- 1/4 cup chopped fresh cilantro
- 1 jalapeño, seeded and finely chopped (optional, for heat)
- Juice of 2 limes
- 2 tablespoons mayonnaise
- 1 tablespoon honey
- Salt and black pepper to taste

For Serving:

- 8 small corn or flour tortillas
- Avocado slices
- Additional lime wedges
- Hot sauce (optional)

Instructions:

Prepare the Grilled Fish:
- Preheat the grill to medium-high heat.
- In a bowl, mix together olive oil, ground cumin, chili powder, garlic powder, onion powder, salt, black pepper, and lime juice to create a marinade.
- Brush the fish fillets with the marinade on both sides.

- Grill the fish for 3-4 minutes per side or until it flakes easily with a fork. Remove from the grill and set aside.

Prepare the Cilantro Lime Slaw:
- In a large bowl, combine shredded green cabbage, shredded purple cabbage, sliced red onion, chopped cilantro, and chopped jalapeño.
- In a separate small bowl, whisk together lime juice, mayonnaise, honey, salt, and black pepper. Pour the dressing over the cabbage mixture and toss until well coated.

Assemble the Tacos:
- Warm the tortillas on the grill for about 20 seconds per side or until pliable.
- Place a grilled fish fillet on each tortilla.
- Top the fish with a generous portion of cilantro lime slaw.
- Add avocado slices on top.

Serve:
- Serve the grilled fish tacos with additional lime wedges and hot sauce on the side.

Enjoy:
- Enjoy these delicious and fresh grilled fish tacos with cilantro lime slaw!

These tacos are perfect for a light and flavorful meal, and the combination of grilled fish with the zesty cilantro lime slaw creates a burst of fresh and vibrant flavors. Serve them at your next gathering for a crowd-pleasing dish!

Baja-Style Fish Tacos

Ingredients:

For the Beer Batter:

- 1 cup all-purpose flour
- 1 teaspoon baking powder
- 1/2 teaspoon salt
- 1 cup cold beer (light and crisp beer works well)

For the Fish:

- 1.5 pounds white fish fillets (tilapia, cod, or mahi-mahi)
- Salt and black pepper to taste
- Vegetable oil for frying

For Assembly:

- Corn tortillas
- Shredded cabbage or lettuce
- Pico de gallo or salsa fresca
- Fresh cilantro, chopped
- Lime wedges
- Crema or sour cream

Instructions:

Prepare the Beer Batter:
- In a bowl, whisk together flour, baking powder, and salt.
- Gradually add the cold beer, whisking continuously until you have a smooth batter. Let the batter rest for 15-20 minutes.

Prepare the Fish:
- Cut the fish fillets into manageable-sized pieces. Pat them dry with paper towels and season with salt and black pepper.
- In a deep skillet or fryer, heat vegetable oil to 350°F (175°C).

Coat the Fish in Batter:
- Dip each piece of fish into the beer batter, ensuring it is well-coated.

Fry the Fish:
- Carefully place the battered fish into the hot oil, a few pieces at a time. Fry until golden brown and crispy, usually 3-4 minutes per side. Remove with a

slotted spoon and place on a plate lined with paper towels to drain excess oil.

Warm the Tortillas:
- Warm the corn tortillas on a dry skillet or griddle for about 20 seconds per side or until pliable.

Assemble the Tacos:
- Place a piece of crispy fish on each tortilla.
- Top with shredded cabbage or lettuce.
- Add a spoonful of pico de gallo or salsa fresca.
- Drizzle with crema or sour cream.
- Garnish with chopped fresh cilantro.
- Serve with lime wedges on the side.

Serve:
- Serve the Baja-style fish tacos immediately.

Enjoy:
- Enjoy the crunchy texture of the beer-battered fish combined with the fresh and vibrant flavors of the toppings.

These Baja-style fish tacos are a perfect blend of crispy, savory, and refreshing elements. They make for a delicious and satisfying meal that captures the essence of Baja California's culinary delights.

Spicy Mango Fish Tacos

Ingredients:

For the Mango Salsa:

- 1 ripe mango, peeled, pitted, and diced
- 1/2 red onion, finely chopped
- 1 jalapeño, seeded and finely chopped
- 1/4 cup fresh cilantro, chopped
- Juice of 1 lime
- Salt and pepper to taste

For the Spicy Fish:

- 1.5 pounds white fish fillets (tilapia, cod, or mahi-mahi)
- 1 tablespoon olive oil
- 1 teaspoon ground cumin
- 1 teaspoon chili powder
- 1/2 teaspoon smoked paprika
- Salt and black pepper to taste
- Corn or flour tortillas

For Assembly:

- Shredded cabbage or lettuce
- Avocado slices
- Lime wedges
- Fresh cilantro, chopped

Instructions:

Prepare the Mango Salsa:
- In a bowl, combine diced mango, finely chopped red onion, jalapeño, cilantro, lime juice, salt, and pepper. Mix well and set aside to let the flavors meld.

Prepare the Spicy Fish:
- Pat the fish fillets dry with paper towels.
- In a small bowl, mix olive oil, ground cumin, chili powder, smoked paprika, salt, and black pepper to create a spice rub.
- Rub the spice mixture onto both sides of the fish fillets.

- Heat a skillet over medium-high heat. Add the fish fillets and cook for 3-4 minutes per side or until the fish is cooked through and flakes easily with a fork.
- Remove the fish from the skillet and break it into smaller pieces.

Warm the Tortillas:
- Warm the tortillas on a dry skillet or in the oven.

Assemble the Tacos:
- Place a portion of the spicy fish onto each tortilla.
- Top with shredded cabbage or lettuce.
- Add a generous spoonful of mango salsa.
- Garnish with avocado slices and chopped fresh cilantro.

Serve:
- Serve the spicy mango fish tacos with lime wedges on the side.

Enjoy:
- Enjoy the vibrant and contrasting flavors of these spicy mango fish tacos!

The combination of spicy fish and sweet mango salsa creates a burst of flavors in every bite. These tacos are perfect for a quick and flavorful meal that's both satisfying and refreshing.

Blackened Fish Tacos with Avocado Crema

Ingredients:

For the Blackened Seasoning:

- 1 tablespoon smoked paprika
- 1 teaspoon dried thyme
- 1 teaspoon onion powder
- 1 teaspoon garlic powder
- 1 teaspoon cayenne pepper (adjust to taste for spiciness)
- 1 teaspoon dried oregano
- 1 teaspoon ground cumin
- Salt and black pepper to taste

For the Avocado Crema:

- 2 ripe avocados, peeled and pitted
- 1/2 cup sour cream or Greek yogurt
- Juice of 1 lime
- 1 clove garlic, minced
- Salt and black pepper to taste

For the Blackened Fish:

- 1.5 pounds white fish fillets (tilapia, cod, or mahi-mahi)
- 2 tablespoons olive oil
- Corn or flour tortillas

For Assembly:

- Shredded cabbage or lettuce
- Pico de gallo or salsa fresca
- Fresh cilantro, chopped
- Lime wedges

Instructions:

Prepare the Blackened Seasoning:
- In a small bowl, mix together smoked paprika, dried thyme, onion powder, garlic powder, cayenne pepper, dried oregano, ground cumin, salt, and black pepper to create the blackened seasoning.

Prepare the Avocado Crema:
- In a blender or food processor, combine peeled and pitted avocados, sour cream or Greek yogurt, lime juice, minced garlic, salt, and black pepper. Blend until smooth and creamy. Adjust the seasoning to taste.

Prepare the Blackened Fish:
- Pat the fish fillets dry with paper towels.
- Rub the blackened seasoning onto both sides of the fish fillets, ensuring they are well-coated.
- Heat olive oil in a skillet over medium-high heat. Cook the fish for 3-4 minutes per side or until blackened and cooked through. Remove from the skillet and break into smaller pieces.

Warm the Tortillas:
- Warm the tortillas on a dry skillet or in the oven.

Assemble the Tacos:
- Spread a layer of avocado crema on each tortilla.
- Place a portion of the blackened fish on top of the crema.
- Top with shredded cabbage or lettuce.
- Add a spoonful of pico de gallo or salsa fresca.
- Garnish with chopped fresh cilantro.

Serve:
- Serve the blackened fish tacos with lime wedges on the side.

Enjoy:
- Enjoy the bold flavors of these blackened fish tacos with creamy avocado crema!

These tacos are a perfect combination of spicy, smoky, and creamy flavors. The blackened seasoning adds a kick to the fish, while the avocado crema provides a cool and refreshing contrast. Serve them at your next taco night for a crowd-pleasing meal!

Beer-Battered Fish Tacos

Ingredients:

For the Beer Batter:

- 1 cup all-purpose flour
- 1 teaspoon baking powder
- 1/2 teaspoon salt
- 1 cup cold beer (light and crisp beer works well)
- 1 egg, beaten

For the Fish:

- 1.5 pounds white fish fillets (tilapia, cod, or mahi-mahi), cut into strips
- Salt and black pepper to taste
- Vegetable oil for frying

For Assembly:

- Corn or flour tortillas
- Shredded cabbage or lettuce
- Pico de gallo or salsa fresca
- Fresh cilantro, chopped
- Lime wedges
- Crema or sour cream

Instructions:

    Prepare the Beer Batter:
- In a bowl, whisk together flour, baking powder, and salt.
- Add the cold beer and beaten egg to the dry ingredients. Whisk until you have a smooth batter. Let the batter rest for about 15-20 minutes.

    Prepare the Fish:
- Pat the fish fillets dry with paper towels.
- Season the fish strips with salt and black pepper.

    Heat the Oil:
- In a deep skillet or fryer, heat vegetable oil to 350°F (175°C).

    Coat the Fish in Batter:
- Dip each fish strip into the beer batter, making sure it's well-coated.

    Fry the Fish:

- Carefully place the battered fish into the hot oil, a few pieces at a time. Fry until golden brown and crispy, usually 3-4 minutes per side. Remove with a slotted spoon and place on a plate lined with paper towels to drain excess oil.

Warm the Tortillas:
- Warm the tortillas on a dry skillet or in the oven.

Assemble the Tacos:
- Place a piece of crispy beer-battered fish onto each tortilla.
- Top with shredded cabbage or lettuce.
- Add a spoonful of pico de gallo or salsa fresca.
- Drizzle with crema or sour cream.
- Garnish with chopped fresh cilantro.

Serve:
- Serve the beer-battered fish tacos immediately, with lime wedges on the side.

Enjoy:
- Enjoy the crispy goodness of these beer-battered fish tacos!

These tacos are a crowd-pleaser and are perfect for a casual and delicious meal. The beer batter adds a light and airy texture to the fish, making each bite satisfyingly crispy. Customize the toppings to your liking and savor the flavors of these classic fish tacos.

Sriracha Mayo Fish Tacos

Ingredients:

For the Sriracha Mayo:

- 1/2 cup mayonnaise
- 2 tablespoons Sriracha sauce (adjust to taste)
- 1 tablespoon lime juice
- Salt to taste

For the Fish:

- 1.5 pounds white fish fillets (tilapia, cod, or mahi-mahi)
- 2 tablespoons olive oil
- 1 teaspoon ground cumin
- 1 teaspoon chili powder
- Salt and black pepper to taste
- Corn or flour tortillas

For Assembly:

- Shredded cabbage or lettuce
- Fresh cilantro, chopped
- Lime wedges
- Avocado slices
- Radishes, thinly sliced (optional)

Instructions:

Prepare the Sriracha Mayo:
- In a bowl, whisk together mayonnaise, Sriracha sauce, lime juice, and salt. Adjust the Sriracha sauce to your desired level of spiciness. Set aside.

Prepare the Fish:
- Pat the fish fillets dry with paper towels.
- In a small bowl, mix olive oil, ground cumin, chili powder, salt, and black pepper. Rub the spice mixture onto both sides of the fish fillets.
- Heat a skillet over medium-high heat. Cook the fish for 3-4 minutes per side or until it flakes easily with a fork. Remove from the skillet and break into smaller pieces.

Warm the Tortillas:

- Warm the tortillas on a dry skillet or in the oven.

Assemble the Tacos:
- Spread a layer of Sriracha mayo on each tortilla.
- Place a portion of the cooked fish on top of the mayo.
- Top with shredded cabbage or lettuce.
- Add avocado slices and radishes (if using).
- Garnish with chopped fresh cilantro.

Serve:
- Serve the Sriracha mayo fish tacos with lime wedges on the side.

Enjoy:
- Enjoy the bold and spicy flavors of these Sriracha mayo fish tacos!

These tacos offer a perfect balance of heat from the Sriracha mayo, freshness from the toppings, and the savory goodness of the spiced fish. They make for a fantastic and satisfying meal with a kick. Adjust the spice level to your liking and savor the deliciousness!

Grilled Mahi-Mahi Tacos with Pineapple Salsa

Ingredients:

For the Grilled Mahi-Mahi:

- 1.5 pounds Mahi-Mahi fillets
- 2 tablespoons olive oil
- 1 teaspoon ground cumin
- 1 teaspoon chili powder
- 1 teaspoon garlic powder
- Salt and black pepper to taste
- Corn or flour tortillas

For the Pineapple Salsa:

- 1 cup fresh pineapple, diced
- 1/2 red onion, finely chopped
- 1 jalapeño, seeded and finely chopped
- 1/4 cup fresh cilantro, chopped
- Juice of 1 lime
- Salt to taste

For Assembly:

- Shredded cabbage or lettuce
- Avocado slices
- Lime wedges
- Sour cream or Greek yogurt (optional)

Instructions:

Prepare the Grilled Mahi-Mahi:
- Preheat the grill to medium-high heat.
- In a small bowl, mix olive oil, ground cumin, chili powder, garlic powder, salt, and black pepper.
- Brush the Mahi-Mahi fillets with the spice mixture on both sides.
- Grill the Mahi-Mahi for 3-4 minutes per side or until it flakes easily with a fork. Remove from the grill and break into smaller pieces.

Prepare the Pineapple Salsa:
- In a bowl, combine diced pineapple, finely chopped red onion, jalapeño, chopped cilantro, lime juice, and salt. Mix well and set aside.

Warm the Tortillas:
- Warm the tortillas on a dry skillet or in the oven.

Assemble the Tacos:
- Place a portion of grilled Mahi-Mahi on each tortilla.
- Top with shredded cabbage or lettuce.
- Add a generous spoonful of pineapple salsa.
- Add avocado slices on top.
- Drizzle with sour cream or Greek yogurt if desired.

Serve:
- Serve the Grilled Mahi-Mahi Tacos with lime wedges on the side.

Enjoy:
- Enjoy the tropical flavors of these Grilled Mahi-Mahi Tacos with Pineapple Salsa!

These tacos offer a combination of smoky grilled Mahi-Mahi, the sweetness of pineapple salsa, and the freshness of the toppings. They're perfect for a summery and light meal. Customize the toppings to your liking and savor the deliciousness!

Cajun Shrimp Tacos with Slaw

Ingredients:

For the Cajun Shrimp:

- 1 pound large shrimp, peeled and deveined
- 2 tablespoons Cajun seasoning
- 1 tablespoon olive oil
- 1 tablespoon lime juice
- Salt and black pepper to taste

For the Slaw:

- 2 cups shredded cabbage or coleslaw mix
- 1/2 cup thinly sliced red onion
- 1/4 cup fresh cilantro, chopped
- 2 tablespoons mayonnaise
- 1 tablespoon lime juice
- Salt and black pepper to taste

For Assembly:

- Corn or flour tortillas
- Avocado slices
- Lime wedges
- Hot sauce (optional)

Instructions:

Prepare the Cajun Shrimp:
- In a bowl, toss the shrimp with Cajun seasoning, olive oil, lime juice, salt, and black pepper. Ensure the shrimp are well-coated.
- Heat a skillet over medium-high heat. Add the seasoned shrimp and cook for 2-3 minutes per side or until they turn pink and opaque. Remove from the heat.

Prepare the Slaw:
- In a separate bowl, combine shredded cabbage or coleslaw mix, thinly sliced red onion, chopped cilantro, mayonnaise, lime juice, salt, and black pepper. Toss until well combined.

Warm the Tortillas:

- Warm the tortillas on a dry skillet or in the oven.

Assemble the Tacos:
- Place a portion of Cajun shrimp on each tortilla.
- Top with a generous amount of slaw.
- Add avocado slices on top.

Serve:
- Serve the Cajun Shrimp Tacos with lime wedges on the side.

Optional:
- Drizzle with hot sauce if you like an extra kick.

Enjoy:
- Enjoy the bold and spicy flavors of these Cajun Shrimp Tacos with Slaw!

These tacos are bursting with Cajun-spiced shrimp and the crisp freshness of slaw. They make for a delicious and satisfying meal, perfect for any day of the week. Customize the toppings according to your preference and savor the flavorful combination!

Chipotle Lime Salmon Tacos

Ingredients:

For the Chipotle Lime Salmon:

- 1 pound salmon fillets, skinless
- 2 tablespoons olive oil
- 2 tablespoons chipotle in adobo sauce, minced
- Zest and juice of 1 lime
- 1 teaspoon ground cumin
- 1 teaspoon chili powder
- Salt and black pepper to taste

For the Avocado Crema:

- 2 ripe avocados, peeled and pitted
- 1/4 cup sour cream or Greek yogurt
- Juice of 1 lime
- Salt and black pepper to taste

For Assembly:

- Corn or flour tortillas
- Shredded lettuce or cabbage
- Sliced radishes
- Fresh cilantro, chopped
- Lime wedges

Instructions:

Prepare the Chipotle Lime Salmon:
- Preheat the oven to 400°F (200°C).
- In a small bowl, mix together olive oil, minced chipotle in adobo sauce, lime zest, lime juice, ground cumin, chili powder, salt, and black pepper.
- Place the salmon fillets on a baking sheet lined with parchment paper. Brush the chipotle lime mixture over the salmon.
- Bake in the preheated oven for 12-15 minutes or until the salmon is cooked through and flakes easily with a fork.

Prepare the Avocado Crema:

- In a blender or food processor, combine peeled and pitted avocados, sour cream or Greek yogurt, lime juice, salt, and black pepper. Blend until smooth and creamy.

Warm the Tortillas:
- Warm the tortillas on a dry skillet or in the oven.

Assemble the Tacos:
- Flake the chipotle lime salmon into bite-sized pieces.
- Spread a layer of avocado crema on each tortilla.
- Place a portion of flaked salmon on top of the crema.
- Top with shredded lettuce or cabbage, sliced radishes, and chopped fresh cilantro.

Serve:
- Serve the Chipotle Lime Salmon Tacos with lime wedges on the side.

Enjoy:
- Enjoy the bold and smoky flavors of these Chipotle Lime Salmon Tacos!

These tacos offer a perfect balance of spicy chipotle, zesty lime, and the richness of salmon. The creamy avocado crema adds a luxurious touch, and the fresh toppings provide a crisp contrast. Customize the toppings according to your liking and savor the deliciousness!

Teriyaki Glazed Tuna Tacos

Ingredients:

For the Teriyaki Glazed Tuna:

- 1 pound sushi-grade tuna, cut into small cubes
- 1/4 cup soy sauce
- 2 tablespoons mirin (sweet rice wine)
- 2 tablespoons sake or dry white wine
- 2 tablespoons brown sugar
- 1 tablespoon sesame oil
- 1 tablespoon grated fresh ginger
- 2 cloves garlic, minced
- 1 tablespoon cornstarch (optional, for thickening)

For the Wasabi Mayo:

- 1/2 cup mayonnaise
- 1 tablespoon soy sauce
- 1 teaspoon wasabi paste (adjust to taste)

For Assembly:

- Corn or flour tortillas
- Shredded Napa cabbage or lettuce
- Sliced cucumber
- Sliced green onions
- Sesame seeds (for garnish)
- Lime wedges

Instructions:

Prepare the Teriyaki Glazed Tuna:
- In a bowl, whisk together soy sauce, mirin, sake or white wine, brown sugar, sesame oil, grated ginger, and minced garlic to create the teriyaki marinade.
- Place the tuna cubes in a shallow dish and pour the teriyaki marinade over them. Let it marinate for at least 15-30 minutes in the refrigerator.

- If you prefer a thicker glaze, mix 1 tablespoon of cornstarch with 2 tablespoons of water. Stir into the teriyaki marinade and heat on the stovetop until it thickens slightly. Allow it to cool.
- Heat a skillet over high heat. Add the marinated tuna cubes and sear for 1-2 minutes per side, or until browned on the outside but still rare in the center.

Prepare the Wasabi Mayo:

- In a small bowl, mix together mayonnaise, soy sauce, and wasabi paste. Adjust the amount of wasabi to your desired level of spiciness.

Warm the Tortillas:

- Warm the tortillas on a dry skillet or in the oven.

Assemble the Tacos:

- Spread a layer of wasabi mayo on each tortilla.
- Place a portion of teriyaki glazed tuna on top of the mayo.
- Add shredded Napa cabbage or lettuce, sliced cucumber, and sliced green onions.

Garnish and Serve:

- Garnish with sesame seeds and serve the Teriyaki Glazed Tuna Tacos with lime wedges on the side.

Enjoy:

- Enjoy the unique and delicious flavors of these Teriyaki Glazed Tuna Tacos!

These tacos offer a delightful combination of sweet and savory teriyaki-glazed tuna with the heat of wasabi mayo. The fresh and crunchy vegetables add a wonderful texture. Customize the toppings according to your liking and savor the delicious fusion of Asian and Mexican flavors!

Soups and Salads Recipes:
Seafood Chowder

Ingredients:

- 2 tablespoons butter
- 1 onion, finely chopped
- 2 celery stalks, diced
- 2 carrots, diced
- 2 cloves garlic, minced
- 1/4 cup all-purpose flour
- 4 cups seafood or fish stock
- 1 cup potatoes, peeled and diced
- 1 bay leaf
- 1 teaspoon dried thyme
- Salt and black pepper to taste
- 1 cup whole milk
- 1 cup heavy cream
- 1 pound mixed seafood (shrimp, scallops, fish fillets, etc.), cut into bite-sized pieces
- Fresh parsley, chopped (for garnish)
- Crusty bread or oyster crackers (for serving)

Instructions:

Sauté Vegetables:
- In a large pot, melt the butter over medium heat. Add chopped onion, diced celery, and diced carrots. Sauté until the vegetables are softened, about 5 minutes.

Add Garlic and Flour:
- Add minced garlic to the pot and cook for another minute until fragrant. Sprinkle the flour over the vegetables and stir well to create a roux.

Pour in Stock:
- Gradually pour in the seafood or fish stock while stirring constantly to avoid lumps. Continue stirring until the mixture thickens.

Add Potatoes and Seasonings:
- Add diced potatoes, bay leaf, dried thyme, salt, and black pepper. Simmer until the potatoes are tender, about 15-20 minutes.

Incorporate Dairy:

- Pour in the whole milk and heavy cream, stirring continuously. Simmer for an additional 10 minutes to allow the flavors to meld.

Add Seafood:
- Gently add the mixed seafood to the chowder. Cook for 5-7 minutes or until the seafood is cooked through. Be careful not to overcook, as seafood cooks quickly.

Adjust Seasoning:
- Taste the chowder and adjust the seasoning as needed. Remove the bay leaf.

Serve:
- Ladle the seafood chowder into bowls. Garnish with chopped fresh parsley.

Enjoy:
- Serve the seafood chowder hot, accompanied by crusty bread or oyster crackers.

Feel free to customize this recipe by adding your favorite seafood or adjusting the thickness of the chowder to your liking. It's a versatile dish that brings the rich flavors of the sea into a comforting bowl of warmth.

Thai Coconut Seafood Soup

Ingredients:

For the Soup Base:

- 1 can (14 ounces) coconut milk
- 4 cups chicken or seafood broth
- 2 stalks lemongrass, smashed and cut into pieces
- 4-5 kaffir lime leaves, torn into pieces (substitute with lime zest if unavailable)
- 3 slices galangal or ginger
- 2 Thai bird chilies, smashed (adjust to taste)
- 2 tablespoons fish sauce (adjust to taste)
- 1 tablespoon soy sauce
- 1 tablespoon brown sugar

For the Seafood:

- 1/2 pound shrimp, peeled and deveined
- 1/2 pound squid, cleaned and sliced into rings
- 1/2 pound mussels or clams, cleaned
- 1/2 pound white fish fillets, cut into bite-sized pieces

Vegetables and Garnishes:

- 1 cup mushrooms, sliced
- 1 medium tomato, cut into wedges
- 1 small onion, sliced
- Fresh cilantro, chopped (for garnish)
- Lime wedges (for serving)

Instructions:

Prepare the Soup Base:
- In a pot, combine coconut milk, chicken or seafood broth, lemongrass, kaffir lime leaves, galangal or ginger, Thai bird chilies, fish sauce, soy sauce, and brown sugar. Bring to a gentle simmer over medium heat.

Add Seafood:
- Once the soup base is simmering, add shrimp, squid, mussels or clams, and white fish fillets. Cook until the seafood is cooked through, and the mussels or clams have opened (discard any that do not open).

Incorporate Vegetables:
- Add sliced mushrooms, tomato wedges, and sliced onion to the soup. Simmer for an additional 5-7 minutes until the vegetables are tender.

Adjust Seasoning:
- Taste the soup and adjust the seasoning by adding more fish sauce or soy sauce if needed. Remove lemongrass stalks, kaffir lime leaves, and galangal slices.

Serve:
- Ladle the Thai Coconut Seafood Soup into bowls. Garnish with fresh cilantro.

Enjoy:
- Serve the soup hot, accompanied by lime wedges for squeezing.

This Thai Coconut Seafood Soup offers a harmonious balance of creamy coconut milk, aromatic herbs, and a medley of seafood. It's a comforting and satisfying dish with a delightful mix of sweet, salty, sour, and spicy flavors. Enjoy the taste of Thailand in a bowl!

Mediterranean Fish Soup

Ingredients:

For the Soup Base:

- 2 tablespoons olive oil
- 1 onion, finely chopped
- 3 cloves garlic, minced
- 1 fennel bulb, thinly sliced
- 1 leek, sliced (white and light green parts only)
- 1 red bell pepper, diced
- 1 can (14 ounces) diced tomatoes
- 4 cups fish or vegetable broth
- 1 cup dry white wine
- 1 teaspoon dried thyme
- 1 teaspoon dried oregano
- 1 bay leaf
- Salt and black pepper to taste
- Pinch of saffron threads (optional)

For the Seafood:

- 1 pound white fish fillets, cut into chunks (such as cod or halibut)
- 1/2 pound shrimp, peeled and deveined
- 1/2 pound mussels or clams, cleaned
- 1/2 pound calamari rings
- 2 tablespoons fresh parsley, chopped (for garnish)

For Serving:

- Crusty bread or baguette slices

Instructions:

Prepare the Soup Base:
- In a large pot, heat olive oil over medium heat. Add chopped onion, minced garlic, sliced fennel, sliced leek, and diced red bell pepper. Sauté until vegetables are softened, about 5-7 minutes.
- Add diced tomatoes, fish or vegetable broth, white wine, dried thyme, dried oregano, bay leaf, salt, black pepper, and saffron threads if using. Bring the

soup to a simmer and let it cook for about 15-20 minutes to allow the flavors to meld.

Add Seafood:
- Once the soup base has simmered, add chunks of white fish, shrimp, mussels or clams, and calamari rings. Cook for an additional 5-7 minutes or until the seafood is cooked through. Discard any unopened mussels or clams.

Adjust Seasoning:
- Taste the soup and adjust the seasoning if needed. Remove the bay leaf.

Serve:
- Ladle the Mediterranean Fish Soup into bowls. Garnish with chopped fresh parsley.

Enjoy:
- Serve the soup hot, accompanied by crusty bread or baguette slices for dipping.

This Mediterranean Fish Soup is a delightful combination of seafood, vegetables, and aromatic herbs. It captures the essence of Mediterranean cuisine and is perfect for a cozy and flavorful meal. Enjoy the rich broth and the variety of textures from the different seafood elements!

Brazilian Moqueca (Fish Stew)

Ingredients:

For the Fish Marinade:

- 1.5 pounds firm white fish fillets (snapper, cod, or halibut), cut into chunks
- Juice of 2 limes
- Salt and black pepper to taste

For the Moqueca Base:

- 2 tablespoons olive oil
- 1 onion, thinly sliced
- 1 bell pepper, thinly sliced (preferably red or yellow)
- 1 jalapeño or green chili, sliced (remove seeds for less heat)
- 3 cloves garlic, minced
- 1 teaspoon ground cumin
- 1 teaspoon paprika
- 1 can (14 ounces) diced tomatoes, undrained
- 1 can (14 ounces) coconut milk
- 1/2 cup fresh cilantro, chopped
- 1/2 cup fresh parsley, chopped
- Salt and black pepper to taste

For Garnish:

- Sliced green onions
- Fresh cilantro or parsley
- Lime wedges

Instructions:

Marinate the Fish:
- In a bowl, combine fish chunks, lime juice, salt, and black pepper. Let it marinate for at least 15-30 minutes.

Prepare the Moqueca Base:
- In a large pot or skillet, heat olive oil over medium heat. Add sliced onions, bell pepper, jalapeño, and minced garlic. Sauté until the vegetables are softened.
- Add ground cumin and paprika to the vegetables, stirring to coat them in the spices.

- Pour in the diced tomatoes with their juice. Cook for a few minutes until the tomatoes start to break down.
- Add coconut milk to the pot, stirring to combine. Bring the mixture to a gentle simmer.

Add Marinated Fish:
- Carefully add the marinated fish chunks to the simmering coconut-tomato mixture. Ensure the fish is evenly distributed.
- Cover the pot and let it simmer for about 10-15 minutes or until the fish is cooked through and flakes easily.

Season and Garnish:
- Season the Moqueca with salt and black pepper to taste. Stir in fresh cilantro and parsley.
- Garnish with sliced green onions, additional fresh cilantro or parsley, and lime wedges.

Serve:
- Serve the Brazilian Moqueca hot over rice or with crusty bread for soaking up the delicious broth.

Enjoy:
- Enjoy the rich and flavorful Brazilian Moqueca, savoring the combination of coconut, tomatoes, and spices in this comforting fish stew.

Brazilian Moqueca is a dish full of vibrant colors and bold flavors, showcasing the diverse and delicious cuisine of Brazil. It's a perfect dish for seafood lovers looking to experience the taste of coastal Brazil.

Spicy Seafood Ramen

Ingredients:

For the Broth:

- 4 cups seafood or vegetable broth
- 2 cups water
- 3 cloves garlic, minced
- 1 tablespoon ginger, grated
- 2 tablespoons soy sauce
- 1 tablespoon miso paste
- 1 tablespoon gochujang (Korean red pepper paste, adjust to taste)
- 1 tablespoon sesame oil
- 1 teaspoon sugar
- Salt and black pepper to taste

For the Spicy Seafood Ramen:

- 8 ounces ramen noodles
- 1/2 pound shrimp, peeled and deveined
- 1/2 pound squid, cleaned and sliced into rings
- 1/2 pound mussels or clams, cleaned
- 4 green onions, sliced
- 2 cups baby spinach or bok choy, chopped
- 2 boiled eggs, halved (optional)
- Nori sheets, sliced (for garnish)
- Sesame seeds (for garnish)
- Lime wedges (for serving)

Instructions:

Prepare the Broth:
- In a pot, combine seafood or vegetable broth, water, minced garlic, grated ginger, soy sauce, miso paste, gochujang, sesame oil, sugar, salt, and black pepper. Bring the broth to a simmer over medium heat and let it simmer for about 15-20 minutes to allow the flavors to meld.

Cook Seafood:
- Add shrimp, squid, and mussels or clams to the simmering broth. Cook until the seafood is cooked through, and mussels or clams have opened (discard any that do not open).

Prepare Ramen Noodles:
- Cook ramen noodles according to package instructions. Drain and set aside.

Add Vegetables:
- Add sliced green onions and chopped baby spinach or bok choy to the broth. Stir until the greens are wilted.

Assemble the Ramen Bowls:
- Divide the cooked ramen noodles among serving bowls.
- Ladle the spicy seafood broth with vegetables and seafood over the noodles.
- Top each bowl with a boiled egg (if using), sliced nori sheets, sesame seeds, and additional green onions.

Serve:
- Serve the Spicy Seafood Ramen hot, garnished with lime wedges on the side.

Enjoy:
- Enjoy the bold and spicy flavors of this homemade Spicy Seafood Ramen, perfect for warming up on a chilly day!

Feel free to adjust the spice level according to your preference, and customize the toppings based on your favorite ramen bowl elements. This dish brings together the goodness of seafood with the comfort of ramen noodles in a spicy and savory broth.

www.ingramcontent.com/pod-product-compliance
Lightning Source LLC
LaVergne TN
LVHW081550060526
838201LV00054B/1847